NINJA Woodfire

Grill & Smoker for Beginners

1200 Days Easy and Vibrant Ninja Woodfire BBQ Grill Recipes for Woodfire Cooking ,Step By Step Instructions for Home cooking

Nona M. Dixon

CONTENTS

INTRODUCTION

Welcome to the sizzling world of the Ninja Woodfire Grill and Smoker Cookbook! If you're passionate about the art of wood-fired cooking and crave the irresistible flavors that only come from grilling and smoking, then this cookbook is your ultimate companion. With a whopping collection of 1200 delicious recipes, get ready to embark on a culinary journey like no other.

Inside these pages, you'll discover a treasure trove of recipes designed to elevate your outdoor cooking experience. From succulent grilled steaks to fall-off-the-bone smoked ribs, from aromatic wood-fired pizzas to mouthwatering smoked salmon, the possibilities are endless. With our cookbook as your guide, you'll unlock the full potential of your Ninja Woodfire Grill and Smoker, and master the art of creating exceptional wood-fired dishes.

But this cookbook isn't just about tantalizing recipes. We've also included comprehensive cooking techniques, tips, and tricks to help you become a true wood-fired cooking aficionado. Whether you're a seasoned grill master or a novice backyard chef, you'll find step-by-step instructions, temperature guides, and practical advice to ensure your success with every dish.

From direct grilling over an open flame to slow smoking meats to perfection, our cookbook covers it all. We've carefully curated recipes that cater to a range of tastes and dietary preferences, including meat lovers, seafood enthusiasts, vegetarians, and those with a sweet tooth. Get ready to impress your family and friends with flavor-packed meals that will leave them craving for more.

So, grab your apron, fire up your Ninja Woodfire Grill and Smoker, and dive into this culinary adventure. It's time to unleash your inner chef, experiment with flavors, and create unforgettable wood-fired dishes that will make every mealtime a celebration. Get ready to become a true master of the grill and smoker with the Ninja Woodfire Grill and Smoker Cookbook - your passport to flavor-packed excellence!

What is Ninja Woodfire Grills and Smokers?

Ninja Woodfire Grills and Smokers are innovative outdoor cooking appliances designed to bring the authentic flavors of wood-fired cooking to your backyard. These grills and smokers use a combination of direct heat from a wood fire and indirect heat from convection to cook your food to perfection.

Here's how Ninja Woodfire Grills and Smokers work:

Firebox: The grill features a firebox where you can load wood or charcoal to generate heat and smoke. The type of wood used can add distinct flavors to your food, such as mesquite, hickory, or applewood.

Heat and Smoke Circulation: The firebox heats up and creates smoke, which is then circulated around the cooking chamber by a fan or natural convection. This creates an even heat distribution and infuses your food with delicious smoky flavors.

Cooking Chamber: The cooking chamber is where you place your food. It can have multiple cooking racks or grates to accommodate different types and sizes of food. The temperature inside the chamber can be controlled using dampers or vents to adjust the airflow and heat.

Direct and Indirect Cooking: Ninja Woodfire Grills and Smokers allow for both direct and indirect cooking. Direct cooking is done over the fire, providing a searing heat for meats or achieving a crispy texture on vegetables. Indirect cooking is done away from the fire, utilizing the circulating heat and smoke to cook food slowly and evenly.

Temperature Control: These grills and smokers typically have built-in thermometers or temperature gauges to monitor the cooking temperature. Some models even offer digital controls for precise temperature adjustments.

Versatility: Ninja Woodfire Grills and Smokers are versatile and can be used for various cooking methods. You can grill steaks, burgers, or vegetables directly over the fire, smoke ribs or briskets low and slow, bake pizzas, roast meats, or even use them as a traditional charcoal grill.

By harnessing the power of wood fire and smoke, Ninja Woodfire Grills and Smokers create a unique and delicious cooking experience, infusing your food with rich, smoky flavors that are sure to impress your family and friends.

When using a Ninja wood-fired grill and smoker, understanding the difference between direct and indirect cooking techniques is essential. Here's a breakdown of each method:

Direct Cooking: Direct cooking involves placing the food directly over the fire or heat source. This method is ideal for quickly searing or grilling foods that benefit from high heat and a direct flame. It creates a charred exterior while locking in juices, resulting in a flavorful crust and a tender interior. Direct cooking is perfect for cooking steaks, burgers, hot dogs, vegetables, and other small or thin cuts of meat.

Indirect Cooking: Indirect cooking involves placing the food away from the direct heat source. Instead of being directly exposed to flames, the food cooks by utilizing the circulating heat and smoke within the cooking chamber. This method is ideal for slow cooking larger cuts of meat, such as roasts, whole chickens, ribs, or briskets. Indirect cooking allows for even and gentle heat distribution, resulting in tender, juicy, and well-cooked meats. It's also suitable for baking, smoking, and roasting vegetables or delicate foods that may burn easily if exposed to direct heat.

By understanding and utilizing both direct and indirect cooking methods with your Ninja wood-fired grill and smoker, you can achieve a wide range of cooking techniques and flavors, from quick sears to slow, smoky barbecues. It provides versatility and allows you to create a variety of dishes that cater to different cooking preferences and desired outcomes.

Breakfastst

Everything Bagel Breakfast Bake

Servings: 4 | Cooking Time: 25 Minutes

Ingredients:
- 6 large eggs
- 2 cups milk
- ½ cup heavy (whipping) cream
- 4 everything bagels, cut into 1-inch cubes (or bagel flavor of choice)
- 2 cups cherry tomatoes
- 1 pound cream cheese, cut into cubes

Directions:
1. In a large bowl, whisk together the eggs, milk, and heavy cream.
2. Add the bagel cubes to the egg mixture. Set aside to rest for 25 minutes.
3. After 25 minutes, insert the Cooking Pot and close the hood. Select BAKE, set the temperature to 375°F, and set the time to 25 minutes. Select START/STOP to begin preheating.
4. While the unit is preheating, slice the cherry tomatoes into thirds.
5. When the unit beeps to signify it has preheated, pour the bagel mixture into the Cooking Pot. Top with the sliced cherry tomatoes and evenly place the cream cheese cubes over the top. Close the hood and bake for 25 minutes.
6. When cooking is complete, remove the pot from the grill and serve.

Banana Churros With Oatmeal

Servings: 2 | Cooking Time: 15 Minutes

Ingredients:
- For the Churros:
- 1 large yellow banana, peeled, cut in half lengthwise, then cut in half widthwise
- 2 tablespoons whole-wheat pastry flour
- ⅛ teaspoon sea salt
- 2 teaspoons oil (sunflower or melted coconut)
- 1 teaspoon water
- Cooking spray
- 1 tablespoon coconut sugar
- ½ teaspoon cinnamon
- For the Oatmeal:
- ¾ cup rolled oats
- 1½ cups water

Directions:
1. To make the churros
2. Put the 4 banana pieces in a medium-size bowl and add the flour and salt. Stir gently. Add the oil and water. Stir gently until evenly mixed. You may need to press some coating onto the banana pieces.
3. Spray the Crisper Basket with the oil spray. Put the banana pieces in the Crisper Basket and AIR CRISP for 5 minutes. Remove, gently turn over, and AIR CRISP for another 5 minutes or until browned.
4. In a medium bowl, add the coconut sugar and cinnamon and stir to combine. When the banana pieces are nicely browned, spray with the oil and place in the cinnamon-sugar bowl. Toss gently with a spatula to coat the banana pieces with the mixture.
5. To make the oatmeal
6. While the bananas are cooking, make the oatmeal. In a medium pot, bring the oats and water to a boil, then reduce to low heat. Simmer, stirring often, until all the water is absorbed, about 5 minutes. Put the oatmeal into two bowls.
7. Top the oatmeal with the coated banana pieces and serve immediately.

Cinnamon Toast With Strawberries

Servings: 4 | Cooking Time: 10 Minutes

Ingredients:

- 1 can full-fat coconut milk, refrigerated overnight
- ½ tablespoon powdered sugar
- 1½ teaspoons vanilla extract, divided
- 1 cup halved strawberries
- 1 tablespoon maple syrup, plus more for garnish
- 1 tablespoon brown sugar, divided
- ¾ cup lite coconut milk
- 2 large eggs
- ½ teaspoon ground cinnamon
- 2 tablespoons unsalted butter, at room temperature
- 4 slices challah bread

Directions:

1. Turn the chilled can of full-fat coconut milk upside down (do not shake the can), open the bottom, and pour out the liquid coconut water. Scoop the remaining solid coconut cream into a medium bowl. Using an electric hand mixer, whip the cream for 3 to 5 minutes, until soft peaks form.
2. Add the powdered sugar and ½ teaspoon of the vanilla to the coconut cream, and whip it again until creamy. Place the bowl in the refrigerator.
3. Insert the Grill Grate and close the hood. Select GRILL, set the temperature to MAX, and set the time to 15 minutes. Select START/STOP to begin preheating.
4. While the unit is preheating, combine the strawberries with the maple syrup and toss to coat evenly. Sprinkle evenly with ½ tablespoon of the brown sugar.
5. In a large shallow bowl, whisk together the lite coconut milk, eggs, the remaining 1 teaspoon of vanilla, and cinnamon.
6. When the unit beeps to signify it has preheated, place the strawberries on the Grill Grate. Gently press the fruit down to maximize grill marks. Close the hood and GRILL for 4 minutes without flipping.
7. Meanwhile, butter each slice of bread on both sides. Place one slice in the egg mixture and let it soak for 1 minute. Flip the slice over and soak it for another minute. Repeat with the remaining bread slices. Sprinkle each side of the toast with the remaining ½ tablespoon of brown sugar.
8. After 4 minutes, remove the strawberries from the grill and set aside. Decrease the temperature to HIGH. Place the bread on the Grill Grate; close the hood and GRILL for 4 to 6 minutes until golden and caramelized. Check often to ensure desired doneness.
9. Place the toast on a plate and top with the strawberries and whipped coconut cream. Drizzle with maple syrup, if desired.

Chicken Breakfast Sausages

Servings:8 | Cooking Time: 8 To 12 Minutes

Ingredients:

- 1 Granny Smith apple, peeled and finely chopped
- 2 tablespoons apple juice
- 2 garlic cloves, minced
- 1 egg white
- ⅓ cup minced onion
- 3 tablespoons ground almonds
- ⅛ teaspoon freshly ground black pepper
- 1 pound ground chicken breast

Directions:

1. Insert the Crisper Basket and close the hood. Select AIR CRISP, set the temperature to 330°F, and set the time to 12 minutes. Select START/STOP to begin preheating.
2. Combine all the ingredients except the chicken in a medium mixing bowl and stir well.
3. Add the chicken breast to the apple mixture and mix with your hands until well incorporated.
4. Divide the mixture into 8 equal portions and shape into patties. Arrange the patties in the Crisper Basket. You may need to work in batches depending on the size of your Crisper Basket.
5. Close the hood and AIR CRISP for 8 to 12 minutes, or until a meat thermometer inserted in the center of the chicken reaches at least 165°F.
6. Remove from the grill to a plate and repeat with the remaining patties.
7. Let the chicken cool for 5 minutes and serve warm.

Banana Chips With Peanut Butter

Servings: 1 | Cooking Time: 8 Hours

Ingredients:
- 2 bananas, sliced into ¼-inch rounds
- 2 tablespoons creamy peanut butter

Directions:
1. In a medium bowl, toss the banana slices with the peanut butter, until well coated. If the peanut butter is too thick and not mixing well, add 1 to 2 tablespoons of water.
2. Place the banana slices flat on the Crisper Basket. Arrange them in a single layer, without any slices touching each another.
3. Place the basket in the pot and close the hood.
4. Select DEHYDRATE, set the temperature to 135ºF, and set the time to 8 hours. Select START/STOP.
5. When cooking is complete, remove the basket from the pot. Transfer the banana chips to an airtight container and store at room temperature.

Spinach With Scrambled Eggs

Servings: 2 | Cooking Time: 10 Minutes

Ingredients:
- 2 tablespoons olive oil
- 4 eggs, whisked
- 5 ounces fresh spinach, chopped
- 1 medium tomato, chopped
- 1 teaspoon fresh lemon juice
- ½ teaspoon coarse salt
- ½ teaspoon ground black pepper
- ½ cup of fresh basil, roughly chopped

Directions:
1. Grease a baking pan with the oil, tilting it to spread the oil around.
2. Select BAKE, set the temperature to 280ºF, and set the time to 10 minutes. Select START/STOP to begin preheating.
3. In the pan, mix the remaining ingredients, apart from the basil leaves, whisking well until everything is completely combined.
4. Place the pan directly in the pot. Close the hood and BAKE for 10 minutes.
5. Top with fresh basil leaves before serving.

Mixed Berry Dutch Baby Pancake

Servings: 4 | Cooking Time: 12 To 16 Minutes

Ingredients:
- 1 tablespoon unsalted butter, at room temperature
- 1 egg
- 2 egg whites
- ½ cup 2% milk
- ½ cup whole-wheat pastry flour
- 1 teaspoon pure vanilla extract
- 1 cup sliced fresh strawberries
- ½ cup fresh raspberries
- ½ cup fresh blueberries

Directions:
1. Select BAKE, set the temperature to 330ºF, and set the time to 16 minutes. Select START/STOP to begin preheating.
2. Grease a baking pan with the butter.
3. Using a hand mixer, beat together the egg, egg whites, milk, pastry flour, and vanilla in a medium mixing bowl until well incorporated.
4. Pour the batter into the pan. Place the pan directly in the pot. Close the hood and BAKE for 12 to 16 minutes, or until the pancake puffs up in the center and the edges are golden brown.
5. Allow the pancake to cool for 5 minutes and serve topped with the berries.

Grilled Egg And Arugula Pizza

Servings: 2 | Cooking Time: 8 Minutes

Ingredients:
- 2 tablespoons all-purpose flour, plus more as needed
- ½ store-bought pizza dough
- 1 tablespoon canola oil, divided
- 1 cup fresh ricotta cheese
- 4 large eggs
- Sea salt, to taste
- Freshly ground black pepper, to taste
- 4 cups arugula, torn
- 1 tablespoon extra-virgin olive oil
- 1 teaspoon freshly squeezed lemon juice
- 2 tablespoons grated Parmesan cheese

Directions:
1. Insert the Grill Grate and close the hood. Select GRILL, set the temperature to MAX, and set the time to 7 minutes. Select START/STOP to begin preheating.
2. While the unit is preheating, dust a clean work surface with flour. Place the dough on the floured surface and roll it into a 9-inch round of even thickness. Dust your rolling pin and work surface with additional flour, as needed, to ensure the dough does not stick.
3. Brush the surface of the rolled-out dough evenly with ½ tablespoon of canola oil. Flip the dough over and brush with the remaining ½ tablespoon oil. Poke the dough with a fork 5 or 6 times across its surface to prevent air pockets from forming during cooking.
4. When the unit beeps to signify it has preheated, place the dough on the Grill Grate. Close the hood and GRILL for 4 minutes.
5. After 4 minutes, flip the dough, then spoon teaspoons of ricotta cheese across the surface of the dough, leaving a 1-inch border around the edges.
6. Crack one egg into a ramekin or small bowl. This way you can easily remove any shell that may break into the egg and keep the yolk intact. Imagine the dough is split into four quadrants. Pour one egg into each. Repeat with the remaining 3 eggs. Season the pizza with salt and pepper.
7. Close the hood and continue cooking for the remaining 3 to 4 minutes until the egg whites are firm.
8. Meanwhile, in a medium bowl, toss together the arugula, oil, and lemon juice, and season with salt and pepper.
9. Transfer the pizza to a cutting board and let it cool. Top it with the arugula mixture, drizzle with olive oil, if desired, and sprinkle with Parmesan cheese. Cut into pieces and serve.

Spinach Omelet

Servings: 1 | Cooking Time: 10 Minutes

Ingredients:
- 1 teaspoon olive oil
- 3 eggs
- Salt and ground black pepper, to taste
- 1 tablespoon ricotta cheese
- ¼ cup chopped spinach
- 1 tablespoon chopped parsley

Directions:
1. Grease a baking pan with olive oil.
2. Select BAKE, set the temperature to 330ºF, and set the time to 10 minutes. Select START/STOP to begin preheating.
3. In a bowl, beat the eggs with a fork and sprinkle salt and pepper.
4. Add the ricotta, spinach, and parsley and then transfer to the baking pan. Place the pan directly in the pot.
5. Close the hood and BAKE for 10 minutes or until the egg is set.
6. Serve warm.

Chocolate Banana Bread With White Chocolate

Servings: 4 | Cooking Time: 30 Minutes

Ingredients:
- ¼ cup cocoa powder
- 6 tablespoons plus 2 teaspoons all-purpose flour, divided
- ½ teaspoon kosher salt
- ¼ teaspoon baking soda
- 1½ ripe bananas
- 1 large egg, whisked
- ¼ cup vegetable oil
- ½ cup sugar
- 3 tablespoons buttermilk or plain yogurt (not Greek)
- ½ teaspoon vanilla extract
- 6 tablespoons chopped white chocolate
- 6 tablespoons chopped walnuts

Directions:
1. Select BAKE, set the temperature to 310ºF, and set the time to 30 minutes. Select START/STOP to begin preheating.
2. Mix together the cocoa powder, 6 tablespoons of the flour, salt, and baking soda in a medium bowl.
3. Mash the bananas with a fork in another medium bowl until smooth. Fold in the egg, oil, sugar, buttermilk, and vanilla, and whisk until thoroughly combined. Add the wet mixture to the dry mixture and stir until well incorporated.
4. Combine the white chocolate, walnuts, and the remaining 2 tablespoons of flour in a third bowl and toss to coat. Add this mixture to the batter and stir until well incorporated. Pour the batter into a baking pan and smooth the top with a spatula.
5. Place the pan directly in the pot. Close the hood and BAKE for 30 minutes. Check the bread for doneness: If a toothpick inserted into the center of the bread comes out clean, it's done.
6. Remove from the grill and allow to cool on a wire rack for 10 minutes before serving.

Grilled Sausage Mix

Servings: 4 | Cooking Time: 22 Minutes

Ingredients:
- 8 mini bell peppers
- 2 heads radicchio, each cut into 6 wedges
- Canola oil, for brushing
- Sea salt, to taste
- Freshly ground black pepper, to taste
- 6 breakfast sausage links
- 6 hot or sweet Italian sausage links

Directions:
1. Insert the Grill Grate and close the hood. Select GRILL, set the temperature to MAX, and set the time to 22 minutes. Select START/STOP to begin preheating.
2. While the unit is preheating, brush the bell peppers and radicchio with the oil. Season with salt and black pepper.
3. When the unit beeps to signify it has preheated, place the bell peppers and radicchio on the Grill Grate; close the hood and GRILL for 10 minutes, without flipping.
4. Meanwhile, poke the sausages with a fork or knife and brush them with some of the oil.
5. After 10 minutes, remove the vegetables and set aside. Decrease the temperature to LOW. Place the sausages on the Grill Grate; close the hood and GRILL for 6 minutes.
6. Flip the sausages. Close the hood and GRILL for 6 minutes more. Remove the sausages from the Grill Grate.
7. Serve the sausages and vegetables on a large cutting board or serving tray.

Bread Pudding

Servings: 6 To 8 | Cooking Time: 30 Minutes

Ingredients:
- 1 loaf (about 1 pound) day-old French bread, cut into 1-inch cubes
- 3 large eggs
- 4 tablespoons (½ stick) unsalted butter, melted
- 1 cup milk
- ¾ cup heavy (whipping) cream, divided
- 2 cups granulated sugar, divided
- 1 tablespoon cinnamon
- 1 teaspoon vanilla extract
- 8 ounces cream cheese, at room temperature

Directions:
1. Line the inside bottom and sides of the Cooking Pot with aluminum foil. This will wrap the bread pudding, so make sure it fits the sides of the Cooking Pot.
2. Place the bread cubes in the Cooking Pot.
3. In a large bowl, whisk together the eggs, melted butter, milk, ½ cup of heavy cream, 1 cup of sugar, cinnamon, and vanilla. Evenly pour the mixture over the bread cubes. Place another foil layer on top of the bread cubes, then fold over all the foil ends to seal all around. Place the Cooking Pot in the refrigerator for at least 30 minutes, or overnight, for the bread to absorb the liquid.
4. Insert the Grill Grate and close the hood. Select GRILL, set the temperature to HI, and set the time to 30 minutes. Select START/STOP to begin preheating.
5. While the unit is preheating, prepare your frosting. In a large bowl, whisk together the cream cheese, remaining 1 cup of sugar, and remaining ¼ cup of heavy cream until smooth. Set aside.
6. When the unit beeps to signify it has preheated, place the Cooking Pot with the foil-wrapped bread pudding on top of the Grill Grate. Close the hood and cook for 30 minutes.
7. When cooking is complete, remove the pot from the grill. Use grill mitts to carefully open up the top foil lining. Drizzle the frosting over the bread pudding. Allow the bread pudding to cool before serving.

Spinach, Leek And Cheese Frittata

Servings: 2 | Cooking Time: 20 To 23 Minutes

Ingredients:
- 4 large eggs
- 4 ounces baby bella mushrooms, chopped
- 1 cup baby spinach, chopped
- ½ cup shredded Cheddar cheese
- ⅓ cup chopped leek, white part only
- ¼ cup halved grape tomatoes
- 1 tablespoon 2% milk
- ¼ teaspoon dried oregano
- ¼ teaspoon garlic powder
- ½ teaspoon kosher salt
- Freshly ground black pepper, to taste
- Cooking spray

Directions:
1. Select BAKE, set the temperature to 300ºF, and set the time to 23 minutes. Select START/STOP to begin preheating.
2. Lightly spritz a baking pan with cooking spray.
3. Whisk the eggs in a large bowl until frothy. Add the mushrooms, baby spinach, cheese, leek, tomatoes, milk, oregano, garlic powder, salt, and pepper and stir until well blended. Pour the mixture into the prepared baking pan.
4. Place the pan directly in the pot. Close the hood and BAKE for 20 to 23 minutes, or until the center is puffed up and the top is golden brown.
5. Let the frittata cool for 5 minutes before slicing to serve.

Coconut Brown Rice Porridge With Dates

Servings: 1 Or 2 | Cooking Time: 23 Minutes

Ingredients:
- ½ cup cooked brown rice
- 1 cup canned coconut milk
- ¼ cup unsweetened shredded coconut
- ¼ cup packed dark brown sugar
- 4 large Medjool dates, pitted and roughly chopped
- ½ teaspoon kosher salt
- ¼ teaspoon ground cardamom
- Heavy cream, for serving (optional)

Directions:
1. Select BAKE, set the temperature to 375°F, and set the time to 23 minutes. Select START/STOP to begin preheating.
2. Place all the ingredients except the heavy cream in a baking pan and stir until blended.
3. Place the pan directly in the pot. Close the hood and BAKE for 23 minutes until the porridge is thick and creamy. Stir the porridge halfway through the cooking time.
4. Remove from the grill and ladle the porridge into bowls.
5. Serve hot with a drizzle of the cream, if desired.

Nut And Seed Muffins

Servings:8 | Cooking Time: 10 Minutes

Ingredients:
- ½ cup whole-wheat flour, plus 2 tablespoons
- ¼ cup oat bran
- 2 tablespoons flaxseed meal
- ¼ cup brown sugar
- ½ teaspoon baking soda
- ½ teaspoon baking powder
- ¼ teaspoon salt
- ½ teaspoon cinnamon
- ½ cup buttermilk
- 2 tablespoons melted butter
- 1 egg
- ½ teaspoon pure vanilla extract
- ½ cup grated carrots
- ¼ cup chopped pecans
- ¼ cup chopped walnuts
- 1 tablespoon pumpkin seeds
- 1 tablespoon sunflower seeds
- Cooking spray

Directions:
1. Select BAKE, set the temperature to 330°F, and set the time to 10 minutes. Select START/STOP to begin preheating.
2. In a large bowl, stir together the flour, bran, flaxseed meal, sugar, baking soda, baking powder, salt, and cinnamon.
3. In a medium bowl, beat together the buttermilk, butter, egg, and vanilla. Pour into flour mixture and stir just until dry ingredients moisten. Do not beat.
4. Gently stir in carrots, nuts, and seeds.
5. Double up the foil cups so you have 8 total and spritz with cooking spray.
6. Put 4 foil cups in the pot and divide half the batter among them.
7. Close the hood and BAKE for 10 minutes, or until a toothpick inserted in center comes out clean.
8. Repeat step 7 to bake remaining 4 muffins.
9. Serve warm.

Blueberry Dump Cake

Servings: 6 To 8 | Cooking Time: 25 Minutes

Ingredients:
- 3 cups fresh blueberries
- ½ cup granulated sugar
- 1 (16-ounce) box yellow cake mix
- 8 tablespoons (1 stick) unsalted butter, melted

Directions:
1. Select BAKE, set the temperature to 300°F, and set the time to 25 minutes. Select START/STOP to begin preheating.
2. While the unit is preheating, wash and pat dry the blueberries. Then place them and the sugar into the Cooking Pot and mix to coat the fruit with the sugar.
3. In a large bowl, mix together the cake mix and melted butter. Stir until the cake mix is no longer a powder but crumbly like a streusel. Cover the blueberry-sugar mixture with the cake crumble.
4. When the unit beeps to signify it has preheated, place the Cooking Pot in the unit. Close the hood and bake for 25 minutes.
5. Baking is complete when the fresh blueberries have bubbled and the cake crumble is golden brown. Serve.

Brie And Apple Tart

Servings: 4 | Cooking Time: 10 Minutes

Ingredients:
- 1 sheet ready-to-bake puff pastry (thawed, if frozen)
- 1 small apple, cored and thinly sliced
- 3 tablespoons honey
- 1 teaspoon light brown sugar, packed
- 1 (8-ounce) round Brie cheese
- 2 tablespoons unsalted butter, melted

Directions:

1. Insert the Grill Grate and close the hood. Select GRILL, set the temperature to LO, and set the time to 10 minutes. Select START/STOP to begin preheating.
2. While the unit is preheating, unroll the pastry dough on a flat surface. Place the apple slices in the center of the dough. Drizzle the honey over the apples and sprinkle the brown sugar on top. Unwrap the Brie and place it on top of the apple slices. Fold the ends of the pastry around the Brie, similar to wrapping up a package, making sure to fully enclose the Brie and apples. Using a basting brush, brush the pastry all over with the melted butter.
3. When the unit beeps to signify it has preheated, place the pastry on the grill. Close the hood and grill for 10 minutes.
4. When cooking is complete, the pastry will be a nice golden brown. The Brie may leak out while cooking, and this is okay. The filling will be hot, so be sure to let it cool for a few minutes before serving.

Bacon And Broccoli Bread Pudding

Servings: 2 To 4 | Cooking Time: 48 Minutes

Ingredients:
- ½ pound thick cut bacon, cut into ¼-inch pieces
- 3 cups brioche bread, cut into ½-inch cubes
- 2 tablespoons butter, melted
- 3 eggs
- 1 cup milk
- ½ teaspoon salt
- Freshly ground black pepper, to taste
- 1 cup frozen broccoli florets, thawed and chopped
- 1½ cups grated Swiss cheese

Directions:

1. Insert the Crisper Basket and close the hood. Select AIR CRISP, set the temperature to 400°F, and set the time to 10 minutes. Select START/STOP to begin preheating.
2. Put the bacon in the basket. Close the hood and AIR CRISP for 8 minutes until crispy, shaking the basket a few times to help it cook evenly. Remove the bacon and set it aside on a paper towel.
3. AIR CRISP the brioche bread cubes for 2 minutes to dry and toast lightly.
4. Butter a cake pan. Combine all the remaining ingredients in a large bowl and toss well. Transfer the mixture to the buttered cake pan, cover with aluminum foil and refrigerate the bread pudding overnight, or for at least 8 hours.
5. Remove the cake pan from the refrigerator an hour before you plan to bake and let it sit on the countertop to come to room temperature.
6. Select BAKE, set the temperature to 330°F, and set the time to 40 minutes. Select START/STOP to begin preheating.
7. Place the covered cake pan directly in the pot. Fold the ends of the aluminum foil over the top of the pan. Close the hood and BAKE for 20 minutes. Remove the foil and bake for an additional 20 minutes. If the top browns a little too much before the custard has set, simply return the foil to the pan. The bread pudding has cooked through when a skewer inserted into the center comes out clean.
8. Serve warm.

Egg And Bacon Nests

Servings:12 | Cooking Time: 30 Minutes

Ingredients:
- 3 tablespoons avocado oil
- 12 slices bacon
- 12 eggs
- Salt
- Freshly ground black pepper

Directions:
1. Insert the Grill Grate and close the hood. Select GRILL, set the temperature to HI, and set the time to 30 minutes. Select START/STOP to begin preheating.
2. While the unit is preheating, brush the avocado oil in the bottom and on the sides of two 6-cup muffin tins. Wrap a bacon slice around the inside of each muffin cup, then crack an egg into each cup. Season to taste with salt and pepper.
3. When the unit beeps to signify it has preheated, place one muffin tin in the center of the Grill Grate. Close the hood and grill for 15 minutes.
4. After 15 minutes, remove the muffin tin. Place the second muffin tin in the center of the Grill Grate, close the hood, and grill for 15 minutes.
5. Serve immediately or let cool and store in resealable bags in the refrigerator for up to 4 days.

Fried Potatoes With Peppers And Onions

Servings: 4 | Cooking Time: 35 Minutes

Ingredients:
- 1 pound red potatoes, cut into ½-inch dices
- 1 large red bell pepper, cut into ½-inch dices
- 1 large green bell pepper, cut into ½-inch dices
- 1 medium onion, cut into ½-inch dices
- 1½ tablespoons extra-virgin olive oil
- 1¼ teaspoons kosher salt
- ¾ teaspoon sweet paprika
- ¾ teaspoon garlic powder
- Freshly ground black pepper, to taste

Directions:
1. Insert the Crisper Basket and close the hood. Select AIR CRISP, set the temperature to 350ºF, and set the time to 35 minutes. Select START/STOP to begin preheating.
2. Mix together the potatoes, bell peppers, onion, oil, salt, paprika, garlic powder, and black pepper in a large mixing and toss to coat.
3. Transfer the potato mixture to the Crisper Basket. Close the hood and AIR CRISP for 35 minutes, or until the potatoes are nicely browned. Shake the basket three times during cooking.
4. Remove from the basket to a plate and serve warm.

Grit And Ham Fritters

Servings: 6 To 8 | Cooking Time: 20 Minutes

Ingredients:

- 4 cups water
- 1 cup quick-cooking grits
- ¼ teaspoon salt
- 2 tablespoons butter
- 2 cups grated Cheddar cheese, divided
- 1 cup finely diced ham
- 1 tablespoon chopped chives
- Salt and freshly ground black pepper, to taste
- 1 egg, beaten
- 2 cups panko bread crumbs
- Cooking spray

Directions:

1. Bring the water to a boil in a saucepan. Whisk in the grits and ¼ teaspoon of salt, and cook for 7 minutes until the grits are soft. Remove the pan from the heat and stir in the butter and 1 cup of the grated Cheddar cheese. Transfer the grits to a bowl and let them cool for 10 to 15 minutes.
2. Stir the ham, chives and the rest of the cheese into the grits and season with salt and pepper to taste. Add the beaten egg and refrigerate the mixture for 30 minutes.
3. Put the panko bread crumbs in a shallow dish. Measure out ¼-cup portions of the grits mixture and shape them into patties. Coat all sides of the patties with the panko bread crumbs, patting them with the hands so the crumbs adhere to the patties. You should have about 16 patties. Spritz both sides of the patties with cooking spray.
4. Insert the Crisper Basket and close the hood. Select AIR CRISP, set the temperature to 400ºF, and set the time to 12 minutes. Select START/STOP to begin preheating.
5. Place the fritters in the basket. Close the hood and AIR CRISP for 8 minutes. Using a flat spatula, flip the fritters over and AIR CRISP for another 4 minutes.
6. Serve hot.

Asparagus And Cheese Strata

Servings: 4 | Cooking Time: 14 To 19 Minutes

Ingredients:

- 6 asparagus spears, cut into 2-inch pieces
- 1 tablespoon water
- 2 slices whole-wheat bread, cut into ½-inch cubes
- 4 eggs
- 3 tablespoons whole milk
- 2 tablespoons chopped flat-leaf parsley
- ½ cup grated Havarti or Swiss cheese
- Pinch salt
- Freshly ground black pepper, to taste
- Cooking spray

Directions:

1. Select BAKE, set the temperature to 330ºF, and set the time to 19 minutes. Select START/STOP to begin preheating.
2. Add the asparagus spears and 1 tablespoon of water in a baking pan. Place the pan directly in the pot. Close the hood and BAKE for 3 to 5 minutes until crisp-tender. Remove the asparagus from the pan and drain on paper towels. Spritz the pan with cooking spray.
3. Place the bread and asparagus in the pan.
4. Whisk together the eggs and milk in a medium mixing bowl until creamy. Fold in the parsley, cheese, salt, and pepper and stir to combine. Pour this mixture into the baking pan.
5. Place the pan directly in the pot. Close the hood and BAKE for 11 to 14 minutes, or until the eggs are set and the top is lightly browned.
6. Let cool for 5 minutes before slicing and serving.

Fast Coffee Donuts

Servings: 6 | Cooking Time: 6 Minutes

Ingredients:
- ¼ cup sugar
- ½ teaspoon salt
- 1 cup flour
- 1 teaspoon baking powder
- ¼ cup coffee
- 1 tablespoon aquafaba
- 1 tablespoon sunflower oil

Directions:
1. In a large bowl, combine the sugar, salt, flour, and baking powder.
2. Add the coffee, aquafaba, and sunflower oil and mix until a dough is formed. Leave the dough to rest in and the refrigerator.
3. Insert the Crisper Basket and close the hood. Select AIR CRISP, set the temperature to 400ºF, and set the time to 6 minutes. Select START/STOP to begin preheating.
4. Remove the dough from the fridge and divide up, kneading each section into a doughnut.
5. Put the doughnuts in the basket. Close the hood and AIR CRISP for 6 minutes.
6. Serve immediately.

Pb&j

Servings: 4 | Cooking Time: 6 Minutes

Ingredients:
- ½ cup cornflakes, crushed
- ¼ cup shredded coconut
- 8 slices oat nut bread or any whole-grain, oversize bread
- 6 tablespoons peanut butter
- 2 medium bananas, cut into ½-inch-thick slices
- 6 tablespoons pineapple preserves
- 1 egg, beaten
- Cooking spray

Directions:
1. Insert the Crisper Basket and close the hood. Select AIR CRISP, set the temperature to 360ºF, and set the time to 6 minutes. Select START/STOP to begin preheating.
2. In a shallow dish, mix the cornflake crumbs and coconut.
3. For each sandwich, spread one bread slice with 1½ tablespoons of peanut butter. Top with banana slices. Spread another bread slice with 1½ tablespoons of preserves. Combine to make a sandwich.
4. Using a pastry brush, brush top of sandwich lightly with beaten egg. Sprinkle with about 1½ tablespoons of crumb coating, pressing it in to make it stick. Spray with cooking spray.
5. Turn sandwich over and repeat to coat and spray the other side. Place the sandwiches in the Crisper Basket.
6. Close the hood and AIR CRISP for 6 minutes or until coating is golden brown and crispy.
7. Cut the cooked sandwiches in half and serve warm.

Sourdough Croutons

Servings:4 | Cooking Time: 6 Minutes

Ingredients:
- 4 cups cubed sourdough bread, 1-inch cubes
- 1 tablespoon olive oil
- 1 teaspoon fresh thyme leaves
- ¼ teaspoon salt
- Freshly ground black pepper, to taste

Directions:
1. Combine all ingredients in a bowl.
2. Insert the Crisper Basket and close the hood. Select AIR CRISP, set the temperature to 400°F, and set the time to 6 minutes. Select START/STOP to begin preheating.
3. Toss the bread cubes and transfer to the basket. Close the hood and AIR CRISP for 6 minutes, shaking the basket once or twice while they cook.
4. Serve warm.

Avocado Eggs

Servings: 4 | Cooking Time: 10 Minutes

Ingredients:
- 4 ripe avocados, divided
- 3 tablespoons extra-virgin olive oil
- 1 teaspoon salt
- ½ teaspoon freshly ground black pepper
- 8 small eggs
- Hot sauce or salsa, for garnish (optional)

Directions:
1. Insert the Grill Grate and close the hood. Select GRILL, set the temperature to HI, and set the time to 10 minutes. Select START/STOP to begin preheating.
2. While the unit is preheating, cut the avocados in half lengthwise and remove the pits, but leave the skin on. You may need to scoop out some of the green flesh so the egg fits once added. Set the extra flesh aside to use as an additional topping later.
3. In a small bowl, whisk together the olive oil, salt, and pepper. Brush the seasoned olive oil on the flesh of the avocados. Then, crack an egg into the center of each avocado half.
4. When the unit beeps to signify it has preheated, place the avocados on the grill, egg-side up. Close the hood and grill for 10 minutes.
5. Cooking is complete when the egg whites are firm. Remove the avocados from the grill. Garnish with the reserved avocado and top with your favorite hot sauce or salsa, if desired.

Mushroom And Onion Frittata

Servings: 4 | Cooking Time: 10 Minutes

Ingredients:
- 4 large eggs
- ¼ cup whole milk
- Sea salt, to taste
- Freshly ground black pepper, to taste
- ½ bell pepper, seeded and diced
- ½ onion, chopped
- 4 cremini mushrooms, sliced
- ½ cup shredded Cheddar cheese

Directions:
1. In a medium bowl, whisk together the eggs and milk. Season with the salt and pepper. Add the bell pepper, onion, mushrooms, and cheese. Mix until well combined.
2. Select BAKE, set the temperature to 400ºF, and set the time to 10 minutes. Select START/STOP to begin preheating.
3. Meanwhile, pour the egg mixture into the baking pan, spreading evenly.
4. When the unit beeps to signify it has preheated, place the pan directly in the pot. Close the hood and BAKE for 10 minutes, or until lightly golden.

Avocado Quesadillas

Servings: 4 | Cooking Time: 11 Minutes

Ingredients:
- 4 eggs
- 2 tablespoons skim milk
- Salt and ground black pepper, to taste
- Cooking spray
- 4 flour tortillas
- 4 tablespoons salsa
- 2 ounces Cheddar cheese, grated
- ½ small avocado, peeled and thinly sliced

Directions:
1. Select BAKE, set the temperature to 270ºF, and set the time to 8 minutes. Select START/STOP to begin preheating.
2. Beat together the eggs, milk, salt, and pepper.
3. Spray a baking pan lightly with cooking spray and add egg mixture.
4. Place the pan directly in the pot. Close the hood and BAKE for 8 minutes, stirring every 1 to 2 minutes, until eggs are scrambled to the liking. Remove and set aside.
5. Spray one side of each tortilla with cooking spray. Flip over.
6. Divide eggs, salsa, cheese, and avocado among the tortillas, covering only half of each tortilla.
7. Fold each tortilla in half and press down lightly. Increase the temperature of the grill to 390ºF.
8. Put 2 tortillas in Crisper Basket and AIR CRISP for 3 minutes or until cheese melts and outside feels slightly crispy. Repeat with remaining two tortillas.
9. Cut each cooked tortilla into halves. Serve warm.

Poultry

Strawberry-glazed Turkey

Servings: 2 | Cooking Time: 37 Minutes

Ingredients:
- 2 pounds turkey breast
- 1 tablespoon olive oil
- Salt and ground black pepper, to taste
- 1 cup fresh strawberries

Directions:
1. Insert the Crisper Basket and close the hood. Select AIR CRISP, set the temperature to 375°F, and set the time to 37 minutes. Select START/STOP to begin preheating.
2. Rub the turkey bread with olive oil on a clean work surface, then sprinkle with salt and ground black pepper.
3. Transfer the turkey in the basket. Close the hood and AIR CRISP for 30 minutes or until the internal temperature of the turkey reaches at least 165°F. flip the turkey breast halfway through.
4. Meanwhile, put the strawberries in a food processor and pulse until smooth.
5. When the cooking of the turkey is complete, spread the puréed strawberries over the turkey. Close the hood and AIR CRISP for 7 more minutes.
6. Serve immediately.

Stuffed Spinach Chicken Breast

Servings: 6 | Cooking Time: 12 Minutes

Ingredients:
- 6 ounces cream cheese, at room temperature
- 1 teaspoon salt
- ½ teaspoon freshly ground black pepper
- ¼ cup mayonnaise
- 2 teaspoons garlic powder
- ½ cup grated Parmesan cheese
- 3 cups loosely packed spinach
- 1 teaspoon red pepper flakes (optional)
- 6 (6- to 8-ounce) boneless, skinless chicken breasts, butterflied (see here)
- Avocado oil

Directions:
1. Insert the Grill Grate and close the hood. Select GRILL, set the temperature to HI, and set the time to 12 minutes. Select START/STOP to begin preheating.
2. While the unit is preheating, in a large bowl, combine the cream cheese, salt, pepper, mayonnaise, garlic powder, Parmesan cheese, spinach, and red pepper flakes (if using). Spread the mixture inside the chicken breasts evenly. Close the breasts (like a book), enclosing the stuffing. Drizzle both sides of the chicken breasts with avocado oil for a nice coating.
3. When the unit beeps to signify it has preheated, place the chicken breasts on the Grill Grate. Close the hood and grill for 6 minutes.
4. After 6 minutes, open the hood and flip the chicken. Close the hood and cook for 6 minutes more.
5. When cooking is complete, open the hood and remove the chicken breasts from the grill. Serve.

Fried Buffalo Chicken Taquitos

Servings: 6 | Cooking Time: 5 To 10 Minutes

Ingredients:

- 8 ounces fat-free cream cheese, softened
- ⅛ cup Buffalo sauce
- 2 cups shredded cooked chicken
- 12 low-carb flour tortillas
- Olive oil spray

Directions:

1. Spray the Crisper Basket lightly with olive oil spray.
2. Insert the Crisper Basket and close the hood. Select AIR CRISP, set the temperature to 360°F, and set the time to 10 minutes. Select START/STOP to begin preheating.
3. In a large bowl, mix together the cream cheese and Buffalo sauce until well combined. Add the chicken and stir until combined.
4. Place the tortillas on a clean workspace. Spoon 2 to 3 tablespoons of the chicken mixture in a thin line down the center of each tortilla. Roll up the tortillas.
5. Place the tortillas in the Crisper Basket, seam-side down. Spray each tortilla lightly with olive oil spray. You may need to cook the taquitos in batches.
6. Close the hood and AIR CRISP for 5 to 10 minutes until golden brown.
7. Serve hot.

Simple Whole Chicken Bake

Servings: 2 To 4 | Cooking Time: 1 Hour

Ingredients:

- ½ cup melted butter
- 3 tablespoons garlic, minced
- Salt, to taste
- 1 teaspoon ground black pepper
- 1 whole chicken

Directions:

1. Select BAKE, set the temperature to 350°F, and set the time to 1 hour. Select START/STOP to begin preheating.
2. Combine the butter with garlic, salt, and ground black pepper in a small bowl.
3. Brush the butter mixture over the whole chicken, then place the chicken in a baking pan, skin side down.
4. Place the pan directly in the pot. Close the hood and BAKE for 1 hour, or until an instant-read thermometer inserted in the thickest part of the chicken registers at least 165°F. Flip the chicken halfway through.
5. Remove the chicken from the grill and allow to cool for 15 minutes before serving.

Roasted Cajun Turkey

Servings: 4 | Cooking Time: 30 Minutes

Ingredients:

- 2 pounds turkey thighs, skinless and boneless
- 1 red onion, sliced
- 2 bell peppers, sliced
- 1 habanero pepper, minced
- 1 carrot, sliced
- 1 tablespoon Cajun seasoning mix
- 1 tablespoon fish sauce
- 2 cups chicken broth
- Nonstick cooking spray

Directions:

1. Select ROAST, set the temperature to 360°F, and set the time to 30 minutes. Select START/STOP to begin preheating.
2. Spritz the bottom and sides of the pot with nonstick cooking spray.
3. Arrange the turkey thighs in the pot. Add the onion, peppers, and carrot. Sprinkle with Cajun seasoning. Add the fish sauce and chicken broth.
4. Close the hood and ROAST for 30 minutes until cooked through. Serve warm.

Rosemary Turkey Breast

Servings: 6 | Cooking Time: 30 Minutes

Ingredients:
- ½ teaspoon dried rosemary
- 2 minced garlic cloves
- 2 teaspoons salt
- 1 teaspoon ground black pepper
- ¼ cup olive oil
- 2½ pounds turkey breast
- ¼ cup pure maple syrup
- 1 tablespoon stone-ground brown mustard
- 1 tablespoon melted vegan butter

Directions:
1. Combine the rosemary, garlic, salt, ground black pepper, and olive oil in a large bowl. Stir to mix well.
2. Dunk the turkey breast in the mixture and wrap the bowl in plastic. Refrigerate for 2 hours to marinate.
3. Remove the bowl from the refrigerator and let sit for half an hour before cooking.
4. Spritz the Crisper Basket with cooking spray.
5. Insert the Crisper Basket and close the hood. Select AIR CRISP, set the temperature to 400°F, and set the time to 30 minutes. Select START/STOP to begin preheating.
6. Remove the turkey from the marinade and place in the basket. Close the hood and AIR CRISP for 20 minutes or until well browned. Flip the breast halfway through.
7. Meanwhile, combine the remaining ingredients in a small bowl. Stir to mix well.
8. Pour half of the butter mixture over the turkey breast in the basket. Close the hood and AIR CRISP for 10 more minutes. Flip the breast and pour the remaining half of butter mixture over halfway through.
9. Transfer the turkey on a plate and slice to serve.

Turkey And Cauliflower Meatloaf

Servings: 6 | Cooking Time: 50 Minutes

Ingredients:
- 2 pounds lean ground turkey
- 1⅓ cups riced cauliflower
- 2 large eggs, lightly beaten
- ¼ cup almond flour
- ⅔ cup chopped yellow or white onion
- 1 teaspoon ground dried turmeric
- 1 teaspoon ground cumin
- 1 teaspoon ground coriander
- 1 tablespoon minced garlic
- 1 teaspoon salt
- 1 teaspoon ground black pepper
- Cooking spray

Directions:
1. Select BAKE, set the temperature to 350°F, and set the time to 25 minutes. Select START/STOP to begin preheating.
2. Spritz a loaf pan with cooking spray.
3. Combine all the ingredients in a large bowl. Stir to mix well. Pour half of the mixture in the prepared loaf pan and press with a spatula to coat the bottom evenly. Spritz the mixture with cooking spray.
4. Place the pan directly in the pot. Close the hood and BAKE for 25 minutes, or until the meat is well browned and the internal temperature reaches at least 165°F. Repeat with remaining mixture.
5. Remove the loaf pan from the grill and serve immediately.

Crispy Dill Pickle Chicken Wings

Servings: 4 | Cooking Time: 26 Minutes

Ingredients:

- 2 pounds bone-in chicken wings (drumettes and flats)
- 1½ cups dill pickle juice
- 1½ tablespoons vegetable oil
- ½ tablespoon dried dill
- ¾ teaspoon garlic powder
- Sea salt, to taste
- Freshly ground black pepper, to taste

Directions:

1. Place the chicken wings in a large shallow bowl. Pour the pickle juice over the top, ensuring all of the wings are coated and as submerged as possible. Cover and refrigerate for 2 hours.
2. Insert the Crisper Basket and close the hood. Select AIR CRISP, set the temperature to 390°F, and set the time to 26 minutes. Select START/STOP to begin preheating.
3. While the unit is preheating, rinse the brined chicken wings under cool water, then pat them dry with a paper towel. Place in a large bowl.
4. In a small bowl, whisk together the oil, dill, garlic powder, salt, and pepper. Drizzle over the wings and toss to fully coat them.
5. When the unit beeps to signify it has preheated, place the wings in the basket, spreading them out evenly. Close the hood and AIR CRISP for 11 minutes.
6. After 11 minutes, flip the wings with tongs. Close the hood and AIR CRISP for 11 minutes more.
7. Check the wings for doneness. Cooking is complete when the internal temperature of the chicken reaches at least 165°F on a food thermometer. If needed, AIR CRISP for up to 4 more minutes.
8. Remove the wings from the basket and serve immediately.

Soy-garlic Crispy Chicken

Servings: 4 | Cooking Time: 20 Minutes

Ingredients:

- 20 to 24 chicken wings
- 2 tablespoons cornstarch
- ¼ cup soy sauce
- ½ cup water
- 1 tablespoon sesame oil
- 1 teaspoon peeled minced fresh ginger
- 1 teaspoon garlic powder
- 1 teaspoon onion powder
- 1 tablespoon oyster sauce
- 2 tablespoons honey
- 1 tablespoon rice vinegar
- 1 tablespoon light brown sugar, packed

Directions:

1. Insert the Grill Grate and close the hood. Select GRILL, set the temperature to MED, and set the time to 20 minutes. Select START/STOP to begin preheating.
2. While the unit is preheating, pat the chicken wings dry with a paper towel and place them in a large bowl. Sprinkle the wings with the cornstarch and toss to coat.
3. In a separate large bowl, whisk together the soy sauce, water, sesame oil, ginger, garlic powder, onion powder, oyster sauce, honey, rice vinegar, and brown sugar until the sugar is dissolved. Place half the sauce in a small bowl and set aside.
4. When the unit beeps to signify it has preheated, place the chicken wings on the Grill Grate. Close the hood and cook for 10 minutes.
5. After 10 minutes, open the hood and flip the wings. Using a basting brush, brush the soy-garlic sauce from the small bowl on the chicken wings. Close the hood and cook for 10 minutes more.
6. When cooking is complete, remove the wings from the grill and place in the large bowl with the remaining soy-garlic sauce. Toss and coat the wings with the sauce, then serve.

Maple-teriyaki Chicken Wings

Servings: 4 | Cooking Time: 14 Minutes

Ingredients:
- 1 cup maple syrup
- ⅓ cup soy sauce
- ¼ cup teriyaki sauce
- 3 garlic cloves, minced
- 2 teaspoons garlic powder
- 2 teaspoons onion powder
- 1 teaspoon freshly ground black pepper
- 2 pounds bone-in chicken wings (drumettes and flats)

Directions:
1. Insert the Grill Grate and close the hood. Select GRILL, set the temperature to MEDIUM, and set the time to 14 minutes. Select START/STOP to begin preheating.
2. Meanwhile, in a large bowl, whisk together the maple syrup, soy sauce, teriyaki sauce, garlic, garlic powder, onion powder, and black pepper. Add the wings, and use tongs to toss and coat.
3. When the unit has beeped to signify it has preheated, place the chicken wings on the Grill Grate. Close the hood and GRILL for 5 minutes. After 5 minutes, flip the wings, close the hood, and GRILL for an additional 5 minutes.
4. Check the wings for doneness. Cooking is complete when the internal temperature of the meat reaches at least 165ºF on a food thermometer. If needed, GRILL for up to 4 minutes more.
5. Remove from the grill and serve.

Lemon Parmesan Chicken

Servings: 4 | Cooking Time: 20 Minutes

Ingredients:
- 1 egg
- 2 tablespoons lemon juice
- 2 teaspoons minced garlic
- ½ teaspoon salt
- ½ teaspoon freshly ground black pepper
- 4 boneless, skinless chicken breasts, thin cut
- Olive oil spray
- ½ cup whole-wheat bread crumbs
- ¼ cup grated Parmesan cheese

Directions:
1. In a medium bowl, whisk together the egg, lemon juice, garlic, salt, and pepper. Add the chicken breasts, cover, and refrigerate for up to 1 hour.
2. In a shallow bowl, combine the bread crumbs and Parmesan cheese.
3. Spray the Crisper Basket lightly with olive oil spray.
4. Insert the Crisper Basket and close the hood. Select AIR CRISP, set the temperature to 360ºF, and set the time to 20 minutes. Select START/STOP to begin preheating.
5. Remove the chicken breasts from the egg mixture, then dredge them in the bread crumb mixture, and place in the Crisper Basket in a single layer. Lightly spray the chicken breasts with olive oil spray. You may need to cook the chicken in batches.
6. Close the hood and AIR CRISP for 8 minutes. Flip the chicken over, lightly spray with olive oil spray, and AIR CRISP for an additional 7 to 12 minutes, until the chicken reaches an internal temperature of 165ºF.
7. Serve warm.

Turkey Jerky

Servings: 2 | Cooking Time: 3 To 5 Hours

Ingredients:
- 1 pound turkey breast, very thinly sliced
- 1 cup soy sauce
- 2 tablespoons light brown sugar, packed
- 2 tablespoons Worcestershire sauce
- ½ teaspoon garlic powder
- ½ teaspoon onion powder
- ½ teaspoon red pepper flakes

Directions:
1. In a resealable bag, combine the turkey, soy sauce, brown sugar, Worcestershire sauce, garlic powder, onion powder, and red pepper flakes. Massage the turkey slices so all are fully coated in the marinade. Seal the bag and refrigerate overnight.
2. An hour before you plan to put the turkey in the dehydrator, remove the turkey slices from the marinade and place them between two paper towels to dry out and come to room temperature.
3. Once dried, lay the turkey slices flat in the Crisper Basket in a single layer. Insert the Crisper Basket in the Cooking Pot and close the hood. Select DEHYDRATE, set the temperature to 150°F, and set the time to 5 hours. Select START/STOP.
4. After 3 hours, check for desired doneness. Continue dehydrating for up to 2 more hours, if desired.
5. When cooking is complete, the jerky should have a dry texture. Remove from the basket and serve, or store in a resealable bag in the refrigerator for up to 2 weeks.

Turkey Meatballs With Cranberry Sauce

Servings: 4 | Cooking Time: 20 Minutes

Ingredients:
- 2 tablespoons onion powder
- 1 cup plain bread crumbs
- 2 large eggs
- 2 tablespoons light brown sugar, packed
- 1 tablespoon salt
- 2 pounds ground turkey
- 1 (14-ounce) can cranberry sauce

Directions:
1. In a large bowl, mix together the onion powder, bread crumbs, eggs, brown sugar, and salt. Place the ground turkey in the bowl. Using your hands, mix the ingredients together just until combined (overmixing can make the meat tough and chewy). Form the mixture into 1½- to 2-inch meatballs. This should make 20 to 22 meatballs.
2. Insert the Grill Grate and close the hood. Select GRILL, set the temperature to MED, and set the time to 20 minutes. Select START/STOP to begin preheating.
3. When the unit beeps to signify it has preheated, place the meatballs on the Grill Grate. Close the hood and cook for 10 minutes.
4. After 10 minutes, open the hood and flip the meatballs. Close the hood and cook for 10 minutes more.
5. When cooking is complete, remove the meatballs from the grill. Place the cranberry sauce in a small bowl and use a whisk to stir it into more of a thick jelly sauce. Serve the meatballs with the sauce on the side.

Buttermilk Ranch Chicken Tenders

Servings: 4 | Cooking Time: 10 Minutes

Ingredients:
- 2 cups buttermilk
- 1 (0.4-ounce) packet ranch seasoning mix
- 1½ pounds boneless, skinless chicken breasts (about 3 breasts), cut into 1-inch strips
- 2 cups all-purpose flour
- ¼ teaspoon paprika
- ¼ teaspoon garlic powder
- ¼ teaspoon baking powder
- 2 teaspoons salt
- 2 large eggs
- ¼ cup avocado oil, divided

Directions:
1. In a large bowl, whisk together the buttermilk and ranch seasoning. Place the chicken strips in the bowl. Cover and let marinate in the refrigerator for 30 minutes.
2. Create an assembly line with 2 large bowls. Combine the flour, paprika, garlic powder, baking powder, and salt in one bowl. In the other bowl, whisk together the eggs. One at a time, remove the chicken strips from the marinade, shaking off any excess liquid. Dredge the chicken strip in the seasoned flour, coating both sides, then dip it in the beaten egg. Finally, dip it back into the seasoned flour bowl again. Shake any excess flour off. Repeat the process with all the chicken strips, setting them aside on a flat tray or plate once coated.
3. Insert the Grill Grate and close the hood. Select GRILL, set the temperature to MED, and set the time to 10 minutes. Select START/STOP to begin preheating.
4. While the unit is preheating, use a basting brush to generously coat one side of the chicken strips with half of the avocado oil.
5. When the unit beeps to signify it has preheated, place the chicken strips on the grill, oiled-side down. Brush the top of the chicken strips with the rest of the avocado oil. Close the hood and grill for 5 minutes.
6. After 5 minutes, open the hood and flip the chicken strips. Close the hood and continue cooking for 5 minutes more.
7. When cooking is complete, the chicken strips will be golden brown and crispy. Remove them from the grill and serve.

Spicy Bbq Chicken Drumsticks

Servings: 4 | Cooking Time: 20 Minutes

Ingredients:
- 2 cups barbecue sauce
- Juice of 1 lime
- 2 tablespoons honey
- 1 tablespoon hot sauce
- Sea salt, to taste
- Freshly ground black pepper, to taste
- 1 pound chicken drumsticks

Directions:
1. In a large bowl, combine the barbecue sauce, lime juice, honey, and hot sauce. Season with salt and pepper. Set aside ½ cup of the sauce. Add the drumsticks to the bowl, and toss until evenly coated.
2. Insert the Grill Grate and close the hood. Select GRILL, set the temperature to MEDIUM, and set the time to 20 minutes. Select START/STOP to begin preheating.
3. When the unit beeps to signify it has preheated, place the drumsticks on the Grill Grate. Close the hood and GRILL for 18 minutes, basting often during cooking.
4. Cooking is complete when the internal temperature of the meat reaches at least 165ºF on a food thermometer. If necessary, close the hood and continue grilling for 2 minutes more.

Mini Turkey Meatloaves With Carrot

Servings: 4 | Cooking Time: 20 To 24 Minutes

Ingredients:
- ⅓ cup minced onion
- ¼ cup grated carrot
- 2 garlic cloves, minced
- 2 tablespoons ground almonds
- 2 teaspoons olive oil
- 1 teaspoon dried marjoram
- 1 egg white
- ¾ pound ground turkey breast

Directions:
1. Select BAKE, set the temperature to 400°F, and set the time to 24 minutes. Select START/STOP to begin preheating.
2. In a medium bowl, stir together the onion, carrot, garlic, almonds, olive oil, marjoram, and egg white.
3. Add the ground turkey. With your hands, gently but thoroughly mix until combined.
4. Double 16 foil muffin cup liners to make 8 cups. Divide the turkey mixture evenly among the liners. Transfer to the pot.
5. Close the hood and BAKE for 20 to 24 minutes, or until the meatloaves reach an internal temperature of 165°F on a meat thermometer. Serve immediately.

Glazed Duck With Cherry Sauce

Servings: 12 | Cooking Time: 32 Minutes

Ingredients:
- 1 whole duck, split in half, back and rib bones removed, fat trimmed
- 1 teaspoon olive oil
- Salt and freshly ground black pepper, to taste
- Cherry Sauce:
- 1 tablespoon butter
- 1 shallot, minced
- ½ cup sherry
- 1 cup chicken stock
- 1 teaspoon white wine vinegar
- ¾ cup cherry preserves
- 1 teaspoon fresh thyme leaves
- Salt and freshly ground black pepper, to taste

Directions:
1. Insert the Crisper Basket and close the hood. Select AIR CRISP, set the temperature to 400°F, and set the time to 25 minutes. Select START/STOP to begin preheating.
2. On a clean work surface, rub the duck with olive oil, then sprinkle with salt and ground black pepper to season.
3. Place the duck in the basket, breast side up. Close the hood and AIR CRISP for 25 minutes or until well browned. Flip the duck during the last 10 minutes.
4. Meanwhile, make the cherry sauce: Heat the butter in a nonstick skillet over medium-high heat or until melted.
5. Add the shallot and sauté for 5 minutes or until lightly browned.
6. Add the sherry and simmer for 6 minutes or until it reduces in half.
7. Add the chicken stick, white wine vinegar, and cherry preserves. Stir to combine well. Simmer for 6 more minutes or until thickened.
8. Fold in the thyme leaves and sprinkle with salt and ground black pepper. Stir to mix well.
9. When cooking of the duck is complete, glaze the duck with a quarter of the cherry sauce, then AIR CRISP for another 4 minutes.
10. Flip the duck and glaze with another quarter of the cherry sauce. AIR CRISP for an additional 3 minutes.
11. Transfer the duck on a large plate and serve with remaining cherry sauce.

Lettuce Chicken Tacos With Peanut Sauce

Servings: 4 | Cooking Time: 6 Minutes

Ingredients:
- 1 pound ground chicken
- 2 cloves garlic, minced
- ¼ cup diced onions
- ¼ teaspoon sea salt
- Cooking spray
- Peanut Sauce:
- ¼ cup creamy peanut butter, at room temperature
- 2 tablespoons tamari
- 1½ teaspoons hot sauce
- 2 tablespoons lime juice
- 2 tablespoons grated fresh ginger
- 2 tablespoons chicken broth
- 2 teaspoons sugar
- For Serving:
- 2 small heads butter lettuce, leaves separated
- Lime slices (optional)

Directions:
1. Select BAKE, set the temperature to 350ºF, and set the time to 5 minutes. Select START/STOP to begin preheating.
2. Spritz a baking pan with cooking spray.
3. Combine the ground chicken, garlic, and onions in the baking pan, then sprinkle with salt. Use a fork to break the ground chicken and combine them well.
4. Place the pan directly in the pot. Close the hood and BAKE for 5 minutes, or until the chicken is lightly browned. Stir them halfway through the cooking time.
5. Meanwhile, combine the ingredients for the sauce in a small bowl. Stir to mix well.
6. Pour the sauce in the pan of chicken, then cook for 1 more minute or until heated through.
7. Unfold the lettuce leaves on a large serving plate, then divide the chicken mixture on the lettuce leaves. Drizzle with lime juice and serve immediately.

Spiced Breaded Chicken Cutlets

Servings: 2 | Cooking Time: 11 Minutes

Ingredients:
- ½ pound boneless, skinless chicken breasts, horizontally sliced in half, into cutlets
- ½ tablespoon extra-virgin olive oil
- ⅛ cup bread crumbs
- ¼ teaspoon sea salt
- ¼ teaspoon freshly ground black pepper
- ¼ teaspoon paprika
- ¼ teaspoon garlic powder
- ⅛ teaspoon onion powder

Directions:
1. Insert the Crisper Basket and close the hood. Select AIR CRISP, set the temperature to 375ºF, and set the time to 11 minutes. Select START/STOP to begin preheating.
2. Brush each side of the chicken cutlets with the oil.
3. Combine the bread crumbs, salt, pepper, paprika, garlic powder, and onion powder in a medium shallow bowl. Dredge the chicken cutlets in the bread crumb mixture, turning several times, to ensure the chicken is fully coated.
4. When the unit beeps to signify it has preheated, place the chicken in the basket. Close the hood and AIR CRISP for 9 minutes. Cooking is complete when the internal temperature of the meat reaches at least 165ºF on a food thermometer. If needed, AIR CRISP for up to 2 minutes more.
5. Remove the chicken cutlets and serve immediately.

Dill Chicken Strips

Servings: 4 | Cooking Time: 10 Minutes

Ingredients:
- 2 whole boneless, skinless chicken breasts, halved lengthwise
- 1 cup Italian dressing
- 3 cups finely crushed potato chips
- 1 tablespoon dried dill weed
- 1 tablespoon garlic powder
- 1 large egg, beaten
- Cooking spray

Directions:

1. In a large resealable bag, combine the chicken and Italian dressing. Seal the bag and refrigerate to marinate at least 1 hour.
2. In a shallow dish, stir together the potato chips, dill, and garlic powder. Place the beaten egg in a second shallow dish.
3. Remove the chicken from the marinade. Roll the chicken pieces in the egg and the potato chip mixture, coating thoroughly.
4. Select BAKE, set the temperature to 325°F, and set the time to 10 minutes. Select START/STOP to begin preheating.
5. Place the coated chicken in a baking pan and spritz with cooking spray.
6. Place the pan directly in the pot. Close the hood and BAKE for 5 minutes. Flip the chicken, spritz it with cooking spray, and bake for 5 minutes more until the outsides are crispy and the insides are no longer pink. Serve immediately.

Sweet-and-sour Drumsticks

Servings: 4 | Cooking Time: 23 To 25 Minutes

Ingredients:
- 6 chicken drumsticks
- 3 tablespoons lemon juice, divided
- 3 tablespoons low-sodium soy sauce, divided
- 1 tablespoon peanut oil
- 3 tablespoons honey
- 3 tablespoons brown sugar
- 2 tablespoons ketchup
- ¼ cup pineapple juice

Directions:

1. Insert the Crisper Basket and close the hood. Select BAKE, set the temperature to 350°F, and set the time to 18 minutes. Select START/STOP to begin preheating.
2. Sprinkle the drumsticks with 1 tablespoon of lemon juice and 1 tablespoon of soy sauce. Place in the Crisper Basket and drizzle with the peanut oil. Toss to coat. Close the hood and BAKE for 18 minutes, or until the chicken is almost done.
3. Meanwhile, in a metal bowl, combine the remaining 2 tablespoons of lemon juice, the remaining 2 tablespoons of soy sauce, honey, brown sugar, ketchup, and pineapple juice.
4. Add the cooked chicken to the bowl and stir to coat the chicken well with the sauce.
5. Place the metal bowl in the basket. Bake for 5 to 7 minutes or until the chicken is glazed and registers 165°F on a meat thermometer. Serve warm.

Grilled Cornish Hens

Servings: 4 | Cooking Time: 20 Minutes

Ingredients:
- ½ cup avocado oil
- 1 teaspoon dried oregano
- ½ teaspoon freshly ground black pepper
- 1 teaspoon garlic salt
- 2 tablespoons minced garlic
- 1 teaspoon chopped fresh thyme
- 1 teaspoon chopped fresh parsley
- 1 teaspoon chopped fresh rosemary
- 2 (1-pound) Cornish hens
- 1 large yellow onion, halved
- 4 garlic cloves, peeled

Directions:
1. Plug the thermometer into the unit. Insert the Grill Grate and close the hood. Select GRILL, set the temperature to LO, then select PRESET. Use the arrows to the right to select CHICKEN. The unit will default to WELL to cook poultry to a safe temperature. Select START/STOP to begin preheating.
2. While the unit is preheating, place the Smart Thermometer into the thickest part of the breast of one of the hens. In a small bowl, whisk together the avocado oil, oregano, pepper, garlic salt, minced garlic, thyme, parsley, and rosemary. Cut a few small slits in the skin of each Cornish hen. Rub the seasoning oil all over the skin and between the skin and meat where you made the slits. Place an onion half and 2 garlic cloves inside the cavity of each hen.
3. When the unit beeps to signify it has preheated, place the hens on the Grill Grate. Close the hood and cook.
4. When the Foodi™ Grill tells you, open the hood and flip the hens. Close the hood and continue to cook.
5. When cooking is complete, remove the hens from the grill and let sit for 5 minutes. Serve.

Sriracha-honey Glazed Chicken Thighs

Servings: 4 | Cooking Time: 17 Minutes

Ingredients:
- 1 cup sriracha
- Juice of 2 lemons
- ¼ cup honey
- 4 bone-in chicken thighs

Directions:
1. Place the sriracha, lemon juice, and honey in a large resealable plastic bag or container. Add the chicken thighs and toss to coat evenly. Refrigerate for 30 minutes.
2. Insert the Grill Grate and close the hood. Select GRILL, set the temperature to MEDIUM, and set the time to 14 minutes. Select START/STOP to begin preheating.
3. When the unit beeps to signify it has preheated, place the chicken thighs onto the Grill Grate, gently pressing them down to maximize grill marks. Close the hood and GRILL for 7 minutes.
4. After 7 minutes, flip the chicken thighs using tongs. Close the hood and GRILL for 7 minutes more.
5. Cooking is complete when the internal temperature of the meat reaches at least 165°F on a food thermometer. If necessary, close the hood and continue grilling for 2 to 3 minutes more.
6. When cooking is complete, remove the chicken from the grill, and let it rest for 5 minutes before serving.

Potato Cheese Crusted Chicken

Servings: 4 | Cooking Time: 22 To 25 Minutes

Ingredients:
- ¼ cup buttermilk
- 1 large egg, beaten
- 1 cup instant potato flakes
- ¼ cup grated Parmesan cheese
- 1 teaspoon salt
- ½ teaspoon freshly ground black pepper
- 2 whole boneless, skinless chicken breasts, halved
- Cooking spray

Directions:
1. Insert the Crisper Basket and close the hood. Select BAKE, set the temperature to 325°F, and set the time to 25 minutes. Select START/STOP to begin preheating.
2. Line the Crisper Basket with parchment paper.
3. In a shallow bowl, whisk the buttermilk and egg until blended. In another shallow bowl, stir together the potato flakes, cheese, salt, and pepper.
4. One at a time, dip the chicken pieces in the buttermilk mixture and the potato flake mixture, coating thoroughly.
5. Place the coated chicken on the parchment and spritz with cooking spray.
6. Close the hood and BAKE for 15 minutes. Flip the chicken, spritz it with cooking spray, and bake for 7 to 10 minutes more until the outside is crispy and the inside is no longer pink. Serve immediately.

Lemon And Rosemary Chicken

Servings: 4 | Cooking Time: 15 Minutes

Ingredients:
- 3 pounds bone-in, skin-on chicken thighs
- 4 tablespoons avocado oil
- 2 tablespoons lemon-pepper seasoning
- 1 tablespoon chopped fresh rosemary
- 1 lemon, thinly sliced

Directions:
1. Insert the Grill Grate and close the hood. Select GRILL, set the temperature to LO, and set the time to 15 minutes. Select START/STOP to begin preheating.
2. Coat the chicken thighs with the avocado oil and rub the lemon-pepper seasoning and rosemary evenly over the chicken.
3. When the unit beeps to signify it has preheated, place the chicken thighs on the Grill Grate, skin-side up. Place the lemon slices on top of the chicken. Close the hood and grill for 8 minutes.
4. After 8 minutes, open the hood and remove the lemon slices. Flip the chicken and place the lemon slices back on top. Close the hood and cook for 7 minutes more.
5. When cooking is complete, remove the chicken from the grill and serve.

Blackened Chicken Breasts

Servings: 4 | Cooking Time: 20 Minutes

Ingredients:
- 1 large egg, beaten
- ¾ cup Blackened seasoning
- 2 whole boneless, skinless chicken breasts, halved
- Cooking spray

Directions:
1. Line the Crisper Basket with parchment paper.
2. Insert the Crisper Basket and close the hood. Select AIR CRISP, set the temperature to 360°F, and set the time to 20 minutes. Select START/STOP to begin preheating.
3. Place the beaten egg in one shallow bowl and the Blackened seasoning in another shallow bowl.
4. One at a time, dip the chicken pieces in the beaten egg and the Blackened seasoning, coating thoroughly.
5. Place the chicken pieces on the parchment and spritz with cooking spray.
6. Close the hood and AIR CRISP for 10 minutes. Flip the chicken, spritz it with cooking spray, and AIR CRISP for 10 minutes more until the internal temperature reaches 165°F and the chicken is no longer pink inside.
7. Let sit for 5 minutes before serving.

Turkey Stuffed Bell Peppers

Servings: 4 | Cooking Time: 15 Minutes

Ingredients:
- ½ pound lean ground turkey
- 4 medium bell peppers
- 1 can black beans, drained and rinsed
- 1 cup shredded reduced-fat Cheddar cheese
- 1 cup cooked long-grain brown rice
- 1 cup mild salsa
- 1¼ teaspoons chili powder
- 1 teaspoon salt
- ½ teaspoon ground cumin
- ½ teaspoon freshly ground black pepper
- Olive oil spray
- Chopped fresh cilantro, for garnish

Directions:
1. Insert the Crisper Basket and close the hood. Select AIR CRISP, set the temperature to 360ºF, and set the time to 15 minutes. Select START/STOP to begin preheating.
2. In a large skillet over medium-high heat, cook the turkey, breaking it up with a spoon, until browned, about 5 minutes. Drain off any excess fat.
3. Cut about ½ inch off the tops of the peppers and then cut in half lengthwise. Remove and discard the seeds and set the peppers aside.
4. In a large bowl, combine the browned turkey, black beans, Cheddar cheese, rice, salsa, chili powder, salt, cumin, and black pepper. Spoon the mixture into the bell peppers.
5. Lightly spray the Crisper Basket with olive oil spray.
6. Place the stuffed peppers in the Crisper Basket. Close the hood and AIR CRISP for 10 to 15 minutes until heated through.
7. Garnish with cilantro and serve.

Crispy Chicken Parmigiana

Servings: 4 | Cooking Time: 15 Minutes

Ingredients:
- 2 large eggs
- 2 cups panko bread crumbs
- ½ cup shredded Parmesan cheese
- 1 tablespoon Italian seasoning
- 1 teaspoon garlic powder
- 1½ pounds boneless, skinless chicken breasts (about 3 breasts), halved lengthwise
- 3 cups marinara sauce, hot
- ½ cup grated Parmesan cheese

Directions:
1. Insert the Grill Grate and close the hood. Select GRILL, set the temperature to MED, and set the time to 15 minutes. Select START/STOP to begin preheating.
2. While the unit is preheating, create an assembly line with 2 large bowls. In one bowl, whisk the eggs. In the other bowl, combine the panko bread crumbs, shredded Parmesan cheese, Italian seasoning, and garlic powder. Dip each chicken breast in the egg and then into the bread crumb mix until fully coated. Set the coated chicken on a plate or tray.
3. When the unit beeps to signify it has preheated, place the chicken on the Grill Grate. Close the hood and grill for 8 minutes.
4. After 8 minutes, open the hood and flip the chicken. Close the hood and continue cooking for 7 minutes more.
5. When cooking is complete, remove the chicken from the grill and top with the marinara sauce and grated Parmesan cheese.

Meats

Lechon Kawali

Servings: 4 | Cooking Time: 30 Minutes

Ingredients:
- 1 pound pork belly, cut into three thick chunks
- 6 garlic cloves
- 2 bay leaves
- 2 tablespoons soy sauce
- 1 teaspoon kosher salt
- 1 teaspoon ground black pepper
- 3 cups water
- Cooking spray

Directions:
1. Put all the ingredients in a pressure cooker, then put the lid on and cook on high for 15 minutes.
2. Natural release the pressure and release any remaining pressure, transfer the tender pork belly on a clean work surface. Allow to cool under room temperature until you can handle.
3. Generously spritz the Crisper Basket with cooking spray.
4. Insert the Crisper Basket and close the hood. Select AIR CRISP, set the temperature to 400°F, and set the time to 15 minutes. Select START/STOP to begin preheating.
5. Cut each chunk into two slices, then put the pork slices in the basket.
6. Close the hood and AIR CRISP for 15 minutes or until the pork fat is crispy. Spritz the pork with more cooking spray, if necessary.
7. Serve immediately.

Baby Back Ribs In Gochujang Marinade

Servings: 4 | Cooking Time: 22 Minutes

Ingredients:
- ¼ cup gochujang paste
- ¼ cup soy sauce
- ¼ cup freshly squeezed orange juice
- 2 tablespoons apple cider vinegar
- 2 tablespoons sesame oil
- 6 garlic cloves, minced
- 1½ tablespoons brown sugar
- 1 tablespoon grated fresh ginger
- 1 teaspoon salt
- 4 baby back ribs

Directions:
1. In a medium bowl, add the gochujang paste, soy sauce, orange juice, vinegar, oil, garlic, sugar, ginger, and salt, and stir to combine.
2. Place the baby back ribs on a baking sheet and coat all sides with the sauce. Cover with aluminum foil and refrigerate for 6 hours.
3. Insert the Grill Grate and close the hood. Select GRILL, set the temperature to MEDIUM, and set the time to 22 minutes. Select START/STOP to begin preheating.
4. When the unit beeps to signify it has preheated, place the ribs on the Grill Grate. Close the hood and GRILL for 11 minutes. After 11 minutes, flip the ribs, close the hood, and GRILL for an additional 11 minutes.
5. When cooking is complete, serve immediately.

Bacon-wrapped Scallops

Servings: 4 | Cooking Time: 10 Minutes

Ingredients:
- 8 slices bacon, cut in half
- 16 sea scallops, patted dry
- Cooking spray
- Salt and freshly ground black pepper, to taste
- 16 toothpicks, soaked in water for at least 30 minutes

Directions:

1. Insert the Crisper Basket and close the hood. Select AIR CRISP, set the temperature to 370°F, and set the time to 10 minutes. Select START/STOP to begin preheating.
2. On a clean work surface, wrap half of a slice of bacon around each scallop and secure with a toothpick.
3. Lay the bacon-wrapped scallops in the Crisper Basket in a single layer. You may need to work in batches to avoid over-crowding.
4. Spritz the scallops with cooking spray and sprinkle the salt and pepper to season.
5. Close the hood and AIR CRISP for 10 minutes, flipping the scallops halfway through, or until the bacon is cooked through and the scallops are firm.
6. Remove the scallops from the basket to a plate and repeat with the remaining scallops. Serve warm.

Sausage Ratatouille

Servings: 4 | Cooking Time: 25 Minutes

Ingredients:
- 4 pork sausages
- Ratatouille:
- 2 zucchinis, sliced
- 1 eggplant, sliced
- 15 ounces tomatoes, sliced
- 1 red bell pepper, sliced
- 1 medium red onion, sliced
- 1 cup canned butter beans, drained
- 1 tablespoon balsamic vinegar
- 2 garlic cloves, minced
- 1 red chili, chopped
- 2 tablespoons fresh thyme, chopped
- 2 tablespoons olive oil

Directions:

1. Insert the Crisper Basket and close the hood. Select AIR CRISP, set the temperature to 390°F, and set the time to 10 minutes. Select START/STOP to begin preheating.
2. Place the sausages in the basket. Close the hood and AIR CRISP for 10 minutes or until the sausage is lightly browned. Flip the sausages halfway through.
3. Meanwhile, make the ratatouille: arrange the vegetable slices on the a baking pan alternatively, then add the remaining ingredients on top.
4. Transfer the sausage to a plate. Place the pan directly in the pot. Close the hood and BAKE for 15 minutes or until the vegetables are tender.
5. Serve the ratatouille with the sausage on top.

Brown-sugared Ham

Servings: 6 To 8 | Cooking Time: 30 Minutes

Ingredients:
- 1 (3-pound) bone-in, fully cooked ham quarter
- 3 tablespoons Dijon mustard
- ¼ cup pineapple juice
- ¼ cup apple cider vinegar
- 1 cup light brown sugar, packed
- 1 teaspoon cinnamon
- ½ teaspoon ground ginger

Directions:
1. Plug the thermometer into the unit. Insert the Cooking Pot and close the hood. Select ROAST, set the temperature to 350°F, then select PRESET. Use the arrows to the right to select PORK. The unit will default to WELL to cook pork to a safe temperature. Insert the Smart Thermometer into the thickest part of the ham. Select START/STOP to begin preheating.
2. While the unit is preheating, score the ham using a sharp knife, creating a diamond pattern on top. Brush on the Dijon mustard.
3. In a small bowl, combine the pineapple juice, vinegar, brown sugar, cinnamon, and ginger.
4. When the unit beeps to signify it has preheated, place the ham in the Cooking Pot. Brush some of the glaze over the entire ham, then pour the rest on top so the glaze can seep into the scores. Close the hood to begin cooking.
5. When cooking is complete, the Smart Thermometer will indicate that the desired temperature has been reached. Remove the ham from the pot and let rest for at least 10 minutes before slicing. Serve.

Pork Chops With Creamy Mushroom Sauce

Servings: 6 | Cooking Time: 10 Minutes

Ingredients:
- 1 cup heavy (whipping) cream
- ½ cup chicken broth
- 1 tablespoon cornstarch
- 1 teaspoon garlic powder
- 6 (6-ounce) boneless pork chops
- 8 ounces mushrooms, sliced

Directions:
1. Insert the Grill Grate and close the hood. Select GRILL, set the temperature to HI, and set the time to 10 minutes. Select START/STOP to begin preheating.
2. While the unit is preheating, in a medium bowl, whisk together the heavy cream, chicken broth, cornstarch, and garlic powder.
3. When the unit beeps to signify it has preheated, place the pork chops on the Grill Grate. Close the hood and grill for 5 minutes.
4. After 5 minutes, open the hood and use grill mitts to remove the Grill Grate and the chops. Pour the cream mixture into the Cooking Pot. Put the Grill Grate back into the unit and flip the pork chops. Close the hood and cook for 5 minutes more.
5. When cooking is complete, remove the pork chops from the grill. Use grill mitts to remove the Grill Grate from the unit and stir the cream mixture. Add the sliced mushrooms, close the hood, and let sit for 5 minutes. Pour the creamy mushroom sauce over the pork chops and serve.

Herb And Pesto Stuffed Pork Loin

Servings: 8 | Cooking Time: 15 Minutes

Ingredients:

- 1 (4-pound) boneless center-cut pork loin
- ½ cup avocado oil
- ½ cup grated Parmesan cheese
- 2 tablespoons finely chopped fresh basil
- 1 tablespoon finely chopped fresh parsley
- 1 tablespoon chopped fresh chives
- ½ teaspoon finely chopped fresh rosemary
- 5 garlic cloves, minced

Directions:

1. Butterfly the pork loin. You can use the same method as you would for a chicken breast or steak (see here), but because a pork loin is thicker, you can perform this double butterfly technique: Place the boneless, trimmed loin on a cutting board. One-third from the bottom of the loin, slice horizontally from the side (parallel to the cutting board), stopping about ½ inch from the opposite side, and open the flap like a book. Make another horizontal cut from the thicker side of the loin to match the thickness of the first cut, stopping again ½ inch from the edge. Open up the flap to create a rectangular piece of flat meat.

2. Plug the thermometer into the unit. Insert the Grill Grate and close the hood. Select GRILL, set the temperature to MED, and select PRESET. Use the arrows to the right to select PORK. The unit will default to WELL to cook pork to a safe temperature. Select START/STOP to begin preheating.

3. While the unit is preheating, in a small bowl, combine the avocado oil, Parmesan cheese, basil, parsley, chives, rosemary, and garlic. Spread the pesto sauce evenly over the cut side of each tenderloin. Starting from a longer side, roll up the pork tightly over the filling. Use toothpicks to secure the ends. Insert the Smart Thermometer into the thickest part of the meat.

4. When the unit beeps to signify it has preheated, place the loin on the Grill Grate. Close the hood to begin cooking.

5. When the Foodi™ Grill indicates it's time to flip, open the hood and flip the loin. Close the hood to continue cooking.

6. When cooking is complete, the Smart Thermometer will indicate that the internal temperature has been reached. Open the hood and remove the loin. Let the meat rest for 10 minutes before slicing in between the toothpicks. Serve.

Beef And Scallion Rolls

Servings: 4 | Cooking Time: 10 Minutes

Ingredients:

- 1 pound skirt steak, very thinly sliced (12 slices)
- Salt
- Freshly ground black pepper
- 6 scallions, both white and green parts, halved lengthwise
- 2 tablespoons cornstarch
- ¼ cup water
- ¼ cup soy sauce
- 2 tablespoons light brown sugar, packed
- 1 teaspoon peeled minced fresh ginger
- 1 teaspoon garlic powder

Directions:

1. Insert the Grill Grate and close the hood. Select GRILL, set the temperature to HI, and set the time to 10 minutes. Select START/STOP to begin preheating.

2. While the unit is preheating, season each steak slice with salt and pepper. With one of the longer sides of a steak slice closest to you, place a scallion length at the bottom, and roll away from you to wrap the scallion. Sprinkle cornstarch on the outer layer of the rolled-up steak. Repeat for the remaining steak slices, scallions, and cornstarch.

3. In a small bowl, mix together the water, soy sauce, brown sugar, ginger, and garlic until the sugar is dissolved.

4. When the unit beeps to signify it has preheated, dip each beef roll in the soy sauce mixture and place it on the Grill Grate, seam-side down. Close the hood and grill for 5 minutes.

5. After 5 minutes, open the hood and flip the beef rolls. Brush each roll with the marinade. Close the hood and cook for 5 minutes more.

6. When cooking is complete, remove the beef rolls from the grill and serve.

Mozzarella Meatball Sandwiches With Basil

Servings: 4 | Cooking Time: 10 Minutes

Ingredients:
- 12 frozen meatballs
- 8 slices Mozzarella cheese
- 4 sub rolls, halved lengthwise
- ½ cup marinara sauce, warmed
- 12 fresh basil leaves

Directions:
1. Insert the Crisper Basket and close the hood. Select AIR CRISP, set the temperature to 350°F, and set the time to 10 minutes. Select START/STOP to begin preheating.
2. When the unit beeps to signify it has preheated, place the meatballs in the basket. Close the hood and AIR CRISP for 5 minutes.
3. After 5 minutes, shake the basket of meatballs. Place the basket back in the unit and close the hood to resume cooking.
4. While the meatballs are cooking, place two slices of Mozzarella cheese on each sub roll. Use a spoon to spread the marinara sauce on top of the cheese slices. Press three leaves of basil into the sauce on each roll.
5. When cooking is complete, place three meatballs on each sub roll. Serve immediately.

Bacon-wrapped Stuffed Sausage

Servings: 4 | Cooking Time: 15 Minutes

Ingredients:
- 1 pound ground Italian sausage (not links)
- 1 cup fresh spinach leaves
- ⅓ cup sun-dried tomatoes, drained
- ½ cup shredded provolone cheese
- 14 slices thin-sliced bacon

Directions:
1. Cut off the two corners (small cuts) of a gallon-size resealable plastic bag. (This makes the next part easier.) Place the sausage in the bag, then press the meat until it is evenly flat and fills the entire bag. Using scissors, cut the side seams of the bag, then peel back the top and flip the flattened sausage onto a sheet of parchment paper. Gently pull back and remove the plastic bag.
2. Layer the spinach leaves, sun-dried tomatoes, and provolone cheese evenly across the bottom half of the sausage. Lift up the end of the wax paper, rolling the sausage over the stuffing, and slowly peel back the wax paper as you continue rolling, leaving the sausage roll on the last bit of wax paper.
3. Insert the Grill Grate and close the hood. Select GRILL, set the temperature to HI, and set the time to 15 minutes. Select START/STOP to begin preheating.
4. While the unit is preheating, on a new piece of wax paper, place 7 bacon slices side by side but not touching each other. Place another bacon slice across the 7 slices, weaving it over and under them, creating a basket-weave pattern. Repeat this with the remaining 6 bacon slices. Once the bacon is woven together, carefully place the sausage roll on the bottom portion of the bacon weave. Then, lifting the end of the wax paper under the bacon, roll it up tightly, until the bacon is wrapped around the stuffed sausage.
5. When the unit beeps to signify it has preheated, place the bacon-wrapped sausage roll on the Grill Grate. Close the hood and grill for 8 minutes.
6. After 8 minutes, open the hood and flip the sausage roll. Close the hood and cook for 7 minutes more.
7. When cooking is complete, open the hood and check the sausage roll. If you prefer your bacon crispier, continue cooking to your liking. Remove the sausage from the grill and serve.

Vietnamese Pork Chops

Servings: 2 | Cooking Time: 12 Minutes

Ingredients:
- 1 tablespoon chopped shallot
- 1 tablespoon chopped garlic
- 1 tablespoon fish sauce
- 3 tablespoons lemongrass
- 1 teaspoon soy sauce
- 1 tablespoon brown sugar
- 1 tablespoon olive oil
- 1 teaspoon ground black pepper
- 2 pork chops

Directions:
1. Combine shallot, garlic, fish sauce, lemongrass, soy sauce, brown sugar, olive oil, and pepper in a bowl. Stir to mix well.
2. Put the pork chops in the bowl. Toss to coat well. Place the bowl in the refrigerator to marinate for 2 hours.
3. Insert the Crisper Basket and close the hood. Select AIR CRISP, set the temperature to 400ºF, and set the time to 12 minutes. Select START/STOP to begin preheating.
4. Remove the pork chops from the bowl and discard the marinade. Transfer the chops into the basket.
5. Close the hood and AIR CRISP for 12 minutes or until lightly browned. Flip the pork chops halfway through the cooking time.
6. Remove the pork chops from the basket and serve hot.

Honey-caramelized Pork Tenderloin

Servings: 4 | Cooking Time: 15 To 20 Minutes

Ingredients:
- 2 tablespoons honey
- 1 tablespoon soy sauce
- ½ teaspoon garlic powder
- ½ teaspoon sea salt
- 1 pork tenderloin

Directions:
1. Insert the Grill Grate and close the hood. Select GRILL, set the temperature to MEDIUM, and set the time to 20 minutes. Select START/STOP to begin preheating.
2. Meanwhile, in a small bowl, combine the honey, soy sauce, garlic powder, and salt.
3. When the unit beeps to signify it has preheated, place the pork tenderloin on the Grill Grate. Baste all sides with the honey glaze. Close the hood and GRILL for 8 minutes. After 8 minutes, flip the pork tenderloin and baste with any remaining glaze. Close the hood and GRILL for 7 minutes more.
4. Cooking is complete when the internal temperature of the pork reaches 145ºF on a food thermometer. If needed, GRILL for up to 5 minutes more.
5. Remove the pork, and set it on a cutting board to rest for 5 minutes. Slice and serve.

Potato And Prosciutto Salad

Servings: 8 | Cooking Time: 7 Minutes

Ingredients:
- Salad:
- 4 pounds potatoes, boiled and cubed
- 15 slices prosciutto, diced
- 2 cups shredded Cheddar cheese
- Dressing:
- 15 ounces sour cream
- 2 tablespoons mayonnaise
- 1 teaspoon salt
- 1 teaspoon black pepper
- 1 teaspoon dried basil

Directions:
1. Select AIR CRISP, set the temperature to 350ºF, and set the time to 7 minutes. Select START/STOP to begin preheating.
2. Put the potatoes, prosciutto, and Cheddar in a baking pan. Place the pan directly in the pot. Close the hood and AIR CRISP for 7 minutes.
3. In a separate bowl, mix the sour cream, mayonnaise, salt, pepper, and basil using a whisk.
4. Coat the salad with the dressing and serve.

Pork Chops In Bourbon

Servings: 4 | Cooking Time: 35 Minutes

Ingredients:
- 2 cups ketchup
- ¾ cup bourbon
- ¼ cup apple cider vinegar
- ¼ cup soy sauce
- 1 cup packed brown sugar
- 3 tablespoons Worcestershire sauce
- ½ tablespoon dry mustard powder
- 4 boneless pork chops
- Sea salt, to taste
- Freshly ground black pepper, to taste

Directions:
1. In a medium saucepan over high heat, combine the ketchup, bourbon, vinegar, soy sauce, sugar, Worcestershire sauce, and mustard powder. Stir to combine and bring to a boil.
2. Reduce the heat to low and simmer, uncovered and stirring occasionally, for 20 minutes. The barbecue sauce will thicken while cooking. Once thickened, remove the pan from the heat and set aside.
3. While the barbecue sauce is cooking, insert the Grill Grate into the unit and close the hood. Select GRILL, set the temperature to MEDIUM, and set the time to 15 minutes. Select START/STOP to begin preheating.
4. When the unit beeps to signify it has preheated, place the pork chops on the Grill Grate. Close the hood, and GRILL for 8 minutes. After 8 minutes, flip the pork chops and baste the cooked side with the barbecue sauce. Close the hood, and GRILL for 5 minutes more.
5. Open the hood, and flip the pork chops again, basting both sides with the barbecue sauce. Close the hood, and GRILL for the final 2 minutes.
6. When cooking is complete, season with salt and pepper and serve immediately.

Crispy Pork Tenderloin

Servings: 6 | Cooking Time: 10 Minutes

Ingredients:
- 2 large egg whites
- 1½ tablespoons Dijon mustard
- 2 cups crushed pretzel crumbs
- 1½ pounds pork tenderloin, cut into ¼-pound sections
- Cooking spray

Directions:
1. Spritz the Crisper Basket with cooking spray.
2. Insert the Crisper Basket and close the hood. Select AIR CRISP, set the temperature to 350ºF, and set the time to 10 minutes. Select START/STOP to begin preheating.
3. Whisk the egg whites with Dijon mustard in a bowl until bubbly. Pour the pretzel crumbs in a separate bowl.
4. Dredge the pork tenderloin in the egg white mixture and press to coat. Shake the excess off and roll the tenderloin over the pretzel crumbs.
5. Arrange the well-coated pork tenderloin in batches in a single layer in the Crisper Basket and spritz with cooking spray.
6. Close the hood and AIR CRISP for 10 minutes or until the pork is golden brown and crispy. Flip the pork halfway through. Repeat with remaining pork sections.
7. Serve immediately.

Sweet And Tangy Beef

Servings: 4 | Cooking Time: 12 Minutes

Ingredients:

- For the beef
- 2 pounds top sirloin steak, thinly sliced
- 1 tablespoon cornstarch
- 3 tablespoons avocado oil
- 3 tablespoons soy sauce
- 2 tablespoons oyster sauce
- 1 tablespoon peeled minced fresh ginger
- 1 tablespoon sesame oil
- ½ teaspoon salt
- 1 onion, coarsely chopped
- 1 red bell pepper, coarsely chopped
- For the sweet and tangy sauce
- ½ cup water
- 2 tablespoons ketchup
- 2 tablespoons oyster sauce
- 2 tablespoons light brown sugar, packed
- 1 teaspoon salt
- 1 teaspoon sesame oil
- 1 tablespoon white vinegar
- 1 tablespoon Worcestershire sauce

Directions:

1. Insert the Cooking Pot and close the hood. Select GRILL, set the temperature to HI, and set the time to 12 minutes. Select START/STOP to begin preheating.
2. In a large bowl, combine the beef, cornstarch, avocado oil, soy sauce, oyster sauce, ginger, sesame oil, and salt. Mix well so the beef slices are fully coated.
3. When the unit beeps to signify it has preheated, transfer the beef to the Cooking Pot. Close the hood and cook for 6 minutes.
4. While the beef is cooking, in a small bowl, combine the water, ketchup, oyster sauce, brown sugar, salt, sesame oil, vinegar, and Worcestershire sauce. Stir until the sugar is dissolved.
5. After 6 minutes, open the hood and stir the beef. Add the onion and red bell pepper to the Cooking Pot. Close the hood and cook for 2 minutes. After 2 minutes, open the hood and add the sauce to the pot. Close the hood and cook for 4 minutes more.
6. When cooking is complete, spoon the beef and sauce over white rice, if desired. Serve.

Spicy Pork With Candy Onions

Servings: 4 | Cooking Time: 52 Minutes

Ingredients:

- 2 teaspoons sesame oil
- 1 teaspoon dried sage, crushed
- 1 teaspoon cayenne pepper
- 1 rosemary sprig, chopped
- 1 thyme sprig, chopped
- Sea salt and ground black pepper, to taste
- 2 pounds pork leg roast, scored
- ½ pound candy onions, sliced
- 4 cloves garlic, finely chopped
- 2 chili peppers, minced

Directions:

1. Select AIR CRISP, set the temperature to 400°F, and set the time to 52 minutes. Select START/STOP to begin preheating.
2. In a mixing bowl, combine the sesame oil, sage, cayenne pepper, rosemary, thyme, salt and black pepper until well mixed. In another bowl, place the pork leg and brush with the seasoning mixture.
3. Place the seasoned pork leg in a baking pan. Place the pan directly in the pot. Close the hood and AIR CRISP for 40 minutes, or until lightly browned, flipping halfway through. Add the candy onions, garlic and chili peppers to the pan and AIR CRISP for another 12 minutes.
4. Transfer the pork leg to a plate. Let cool for 5 minutes and slice. Spread the juices left in the pan over the pork and serve warm with the candy onions.

Korean Bbq Beef

Servings: 4 | Cooking Time: 5 Minutes

Ingredients:
- ⅓ cup soy sauce
- 2 tablespoons sesame oil
- 2½ tablespoons brown sugar
- 3 garlic cloves, minced
- ½ teaspoon freshly ground black pepper
- 1 pound rib eye steak, thinly sliced
- 2 scallions, thinly sliced, for garnish
- Toasted sesame seeds, for garnish

Directions:
1. In a small bowl, whisk together the soy sauce, sesame oil, brown sugar, garlic, and black pepper until fully combined.
2. Place the beef into a large shallow bowl, and pour the sauce over the slices. Cover and refrigerate for 1 hour.
3. Insert the Grill Grate and close the hood. Select GRILL, set the temperature to MEDIUM, and set the time to 5 minutes. Select START/STOP to begin preheating.
4. When the unit beeps to signify it has preheated, place the beef onto the Grill Grate. Close the hood and GRILL for 4 minutes without flipping.
5. After 4 minutes, check the steak for desired doneness, grilling for up to 1 minute more, if desired.
6. When cooking is complete, top with scallions and sesame seeds and serve immediately.

Tonkatsu

Servings: 4 | Cooking Time: 10 Minutes Per Batch

Ingredients:
- ⅔ cup all-purpose flour
- 2 large egg whites
- 1 cup panko breadcrumbs
- 4 center-cut boneless pork loin chops (about ½ inch thick)
- Cooking spray

Directions:
1. Spritz the Crisper Basket with cooking spray.
2. Insert the Crisper Basket and close the hood. Select AIR CRISP, set the temperature to 375ºF, and set the time to 10 minutes. Select START/STOP to begin preheating.
3. Pour the flour in a bowl. Whisk the egg whites in a separate bowl. Spread the breadcrumbs on a large plate.
4. Dredge the pork loin chops in the flour first, press to coat well, then shake the excess off and dunk the chops in the eggs whites, and then roll the chops over the breadcrumbs. Shake the excess off.
5. Arrange the pork chops in batches in a single layer in the basket and spritz with cooking spray.
6. Close the hood and AIR CRISP for 10 minutes or until the pork chops are lightly browned and crunchy. Flip the chops halfway through. Repeat with remaining chops.
7. Serve immediately.

Miso Marinated Steak

Servings: 4 | Cooking Time: 12 Minutes

Ingredients:
- ¾ pound flank steak
- 1½ tablespoons sake
- 1 tablespoon brown miso paste
- 1 teaspoon honey
- 2 cloves garlic, pressed
- 1 tablespoon olive oil

Directions:
1. Put all the ingredients in a Ziploc bag. Shake to cover the steak well with the seasonings and refrigerate for at least 1 hour.
2. Insert the Crisper Basket and close the hood. Select AIR CRISP, set the temperature to 400ºF, and set the time to 12 minutes. Select START/STOP to begin preheating.
3. Coat all sides of the steak with cooking spray. Put the steak in the basket.
4. Close the hood and AIR CRISP for 12 minutes, turning the steak twice during the cooking time, then serve immediately.

Simple Pork Meatballs With Red Chili

Servings: 4 | Cooking Time: 15 Minutes

Ingredients:
- 1 pound ground pork
- 2 cloves garlic, finely minced
- 1 cup scallions, finely chopped
- 1½ tablespoons Worcestershire sauce
- ½ teaspoon freshly grated ginger root
- 1 teaspoon turmeric powder
- 1 tablespoon oyster sauce
- 1 small sliced red chili, for garnish
- Cooking spray

Directions:
1. Spritz the Crisper Basket with cooking spray.
2. Insert the Crisper Basket and close the hood. Select AIR CRISP, set the temperature to 350ºF, and set the time to 15 minutes. Select START/STOP to begin preheating.
3. Combine all the ingredients, except for the red chili in a large bowl. Toss to mix well.
4. Shape the mixture into equally sized balls, then arrange them in the basket and spritz with cooking spray.
5. Close the hood and AIR CRISP for 15 minutes or until the balls are lightly browned. Flip the balls halfway through.
6. Serve the pork meatballs with red chili on top.

Peppercorn Beef Tenderloin

Servings: 6 To 8 | Cooking Time: 30 Minutes

Ingredients:
- ¾ cup tricolored peppercorns or black peppercorns, crushed
- 2 garlic cloves, minced
- 2 tablespoons avocado oil
- 1 tablespoon kosher salt
- ¼ cup yellow mustard or horseradish
- 1 (3-pound) beef tenderloin, trimmed

Directions:
1. In a small bowl, combine the crushed peppercorns, garlic, avocado oil, salt, and mustard. Using a basting brush, coat the tenderloin all over with the mustard mixture. Then press the mixture into the meat with your hands.
2. Plug the thermometer into the unit. Insert the Grill Grate and close the hood. Select ROAST, set the temperature to 400°F, then select PRESET. Use the arrows to the right to select BEEF. The unit will default to WELL to cook to a safe temperature. Insert the Smart Thermometer into the thickest part of the loin. Select START/STOP to begin preheating.
3. When the unit beeps to signify it has preheated, place the tenderloin on the Grill Grate. (If the Splatter Shield is touching the tenderloin when you close the hood, use grill mitts to remove the Grill Grate and place the tenderloin in the Cooking Pot instead.) Close the hood and cook until the Smart Thermometer indicates your desired internal temperature has been reached.
4. When cooking is complete, remove the tenderloin and let rest for 10 minutes before slicing and serving.
5. You will want to tuck the thin (tail) end under the center and tie it with kitchen twine or butcher's twine every 2 inches to make a uniform size to get the perfect level of doneness throughout. You can also ask your butcher to tie it for you.

Ranch And Cheddar Pork Chops

Servings: 6 | Cooking Time: 10 Minutes

Ingredients:
- 8 ounces cream cheese, at room temperature
- 1 tablespoon ranch seasoning mix
- ½ cup shredded cheddar cheese
- 6 (6-ounce) boneless pork chops

Directions:
1. Insert the Grill Grate and close the hood. Select GRILL, set the temperature to HI, and set the time to 10 minutes. Select START/STOP to begin preheating.
2. While the unit is preheating, in a small bowl, combine the cream cheese, ranch seasoning, and cheddar cheese.
3. When the unit beeps to signify it has preheated, place the pork chops on the Grill Grate. Close the hood and grill for 5 minutes.
4. After 5 minutes, open the hood and flip the chops. Then top each with the ranch-cheese mixture. Close the hood and cook for 5 minutes more.
5. When cooking is complete, remove the chops from the grill and serve.

Cheesy Jalapeño Popper Burgers

Servings: 4 | Cooking Time: 9 Minutes

Ingredients:
- 2 jalapeño peppers, seeded, stemmed, and minced
- ½ cup shredded Cheddar cheese
- 4 ounces cream cheese, at room temperature
- 4 slices bacon, cooked and crumbled
- 2 pounds ground beef
- ½ teaspoon chili powder
- ¼ teaspoon paprika
- ¼ teaspoon freshly ground black pepper
- 4 hamburger buns
- 4 slices pepper Jack cheese
- Lettuce, sliced tomato, and sliced red onion, for topping (optional)

Directions:
1. Insert the Grill Grate and close the hood. Select GRILL, set the temperature to HIGH, and set the time to 9 minutes. Select START/STOP to begin preheating.
2. In a medium bowl, combine the peppers, Cheddar cheese, cream cheese, and bacon until well combined.
3. Form the ground beef into 8¼-inch-thick patties. Spoon some of the filling mixture onto four of the patties, then place a second patty on top of each to make four burgers. Use your fingers to pinch the edges of the patties together to seal in the filling. Reshape the patties with your hands as needed.
4. Combine the chili powder, paprika, and pepper in a small bowl. Sprinkle the mixture onto both sides of the burgers.
5. When the units beeps to signify it has preheated, place the burgers on the Grill Grate. Close the hood and GRILL for 4 minutes without flipping. Cooking is complete when the internal temperature of the beef reaches at least 145°F on a food thermometer. If needed, GRILL for up to 5 more minutes.
6. Place the burgers on the hamburger buns and top with pepper Jack cheese. Add lettuce, tomato, and red onion, if desired.

Apple-glazed Pork

Servings: 4 | Cooking Time: 19 Minutes

Ingredients:
- 1 sliced apple
- 1 small onion, sliced
- 2 tablespoons apple cider vinegar, divided
- ½ teaspoon thyme
- ½ teaspoon rosemary
- ¼ teaspoon brown sugar
- 3 tablespoons olive oil, divided
- ¼ teaspoon smoked paprika
- 4 pork chops
- Salt and ground black pepper, to taste

Directions:
1. Select BAKE, set the temperature to 350ºF, and set the time to 4 minutes. Select START/STOP to begin preheating.
2. Combine the apple slices, onion, 1 tablespoon of vinegar, thyme, rosemary, brown sugar, and 2 tablespoons of olive oil in a baking pan. Stir to mix well.
3. Place the pan directly in the pot. Close the hood and BAKE for 4 minutes.
4. Meanwhile, combine the remaining vinegar and olive oil, and paprika in a large bowl. Sprinkle with salt and ground black pepper. Stir to mix well. Dredge the pork in the mixture and toss to coat well.
5. Remove the baking pan from the grill and put in the pork. Place the pan directly in the pot. Close the hood and AIR CRISP for 10 minutes to lightly brown the pork. Flip the pork chops halfway through.
6. Remove the pork from the grill and baste with baked apple mixture on both sides. Put the pork back to the grill and AIR CRISP for an additional 5 minutes. Flip halfway through.
7. Serve immediately.

Pork Spareribs With Peanut Sauce

Servings: 6 | Cooking Time: 30 Minutes

Ingredients:
- 2 (2- to 3-pound) racks St. Louis–style spareribs
- Sea salt
- ½ cup crunchy peanut butter
- 1 tablespoon rice vinegar
- 2 tablespoons hoisin sauce
- 1 tablespoon honey
- 2 tablespoons soy sauce
- 1 teaspoon garlic powder

Directions:
1. Plug the thermometer into the unit. Insert the Grill Grate and close the hood. Select GRILL, set the temperature to MED, and select PRESET. Use the arrows to the right to select PORK. The unit will default to WELL to cook the pork to a safe temperature. Insert the Smart Thermometer into the thickest part of the meat between two bones, making sure it does not touch bone. Select START/STOP to begin preheating.
2. When the unit beeps to signify it has preheated, place the racks of ribs on the Grill Grate. Close the hood to begin cooking.
3. When the Foodi™ Grill indicates it's time to flip, open the hood and flip the racks. Then close the hood to continue cooking.
4. While the ribs are cooking, in a small bowl, combine the peanut butter, vinegar, hoisin sauce, honey, soy sauce, and garlic powder and mix until well blended.
5. When cooking is complete, the Smart Thermometer will indicate that the desired internal temperature has been reached. Open the hood and remove the ribs. Either pour the sauce over the ribs or divide the sauce between individual bowls for dipping. Serve.

Easy Beef Schnitzel

Servings: 1 | Cooking Time: 12 Minutes

Ingredients:
- ½ cup friendly bread crumbs
- 2 tablespoons olive oil
- Pepper and salt, to taste
- 1 egg, beaten
- 1 thin beef schnitzel

Directions:
1. Insert the Crisper Basket and close the hood. Select AIR CRISP, set the temperature to 350°F, and set the time to 12 minutes. Select START/STOP to begin preheating.
2. In a shallow dish, combine the bread crumbs, oil, pepper, and salt.
3. In a second shallow dish, place the beaten egg.
4. Dredge the schnitzel in the egg before rolling it in the bread crumbs.
5. Put the coated schnitzel in the Crisper Basket. Close the hood and AIR CRISP for 12 minutes. Flip the schnitzel halfway through.
6. Serve immediately.

Garlic Herb Crusted Lamb

Servings: 6 | Cooking Time: 1 Hour

Ingredients:
- ¼ cup red wine vinegar
- 3 garlic cloves, minced
- 1 tablespoon garlic powder
- 1 tablespoon paprika
- 1 tablespoon ground cumin
- 1 tablespoon dried parsley
- 1 tablespoon dried thyme
- 1 tablespoon dried oregano
- 1 teaspoon salt
- ½ teaspoon freshly ground black pepper
- Juice of ½ lemon
- 1 (3-pound) boneless leg of lamb

Directions:
1. In a large bowl, mix together the vinegar, garlic, garlic powder, paprika, cumin, parsley, thyme, oregano, salt, pepper, and lemon juice until well combined—the marinade will turn into a thick paste. Add the leg of lamb and massage the marinade into the meat. Coat the lamb with the marinade and let sit for at least 30 minutes. If marinating for longer, cover and refrigerate.
2. Plug the thermometer into the unit. Insert the Grill Grate and close the hood. Select GRILL, set the temperature to LO, and set the time to 30 minutes. Insert the Smart Thermometer into the thickest part of the meat. Select START/STOP to begin preheating.
3. When the unit beeps to signify it has preheated, place the lamb on the Grill Grate. Select the BEEF/LAMB preset and choose MEDIUM-WELL or according to your desired doneness. Close the hood and cook for 30 minutes.
4. After 30 minutes, which is the maximum time for the LO setting, select GRILL again, set the temperature to LO, and set the time to 30 minutes. Select START/STOP and press PREHEAT to skip preheating. Cook until the Smart Thermometer indicates that the desired internal temperature has been reached.
5. When cooking is complete, remove the lamb from the grill and serve.

Meatless

Bean And Corn Stuffed Peppers

Servings: 6 | Cooking Time: 32 Minutes

Ingredients:
- 6 red or green bell peppers, seeded, ribs removed, and top ½-inch cut off and reserved
- 4 garlic cloves, minced
- 1 small white onion, diced
- 2 bags instant rice, cooked in microwave
- 1 can red or green enchilada sauce
- ½ teaspoon chili powder
- ¼ teaspoon ground cumin
- ½ cup canned black beans, rinsed and drained
- ½ cup frozen corn
- ½ cup vegetable stock
- 1 bag shredded Colby Jack cheese, divided

Directions:
1. Chop the ½-inch portions of reserved bell pepper and place in a large mixing bowl. Add the garlic, onion, cooked instant rice, enchilada sauce, chili powder, cumin, black beans, corn, vegetable stock, and half the cheese. Mix to combine.
2. Use the cooking pot without the Grill Grate or Crisper Basket installed. Close the hood. Select ROAST, set the temperature to 350ºF, and set the time to 32 minutes. Select START/STOP to begin preheating.
3. While the unit is preheating, spoon the mixture into the peppers, filling them up as full as possible. If necessary, lightly press the mixture down into the peppers to fit more in.
4. When the unit beeps to signify it has preheated, place the peppers, upright, in the pot. Close the hood and ROAST for 30 minutes.
5. After 30 minutes, sprinkle the remaining cheese over the top of the peppers. Close the hood and ROAST for the remaining 2 minutes.
6. When cooking is complete, serve immediately.

Asian-inspired Broccoli

Servings: 2 | Cooking Time: 10 Minutes

Ingredients:
- 12 ounces broccoli florets
- 2 tablespoons Asian hot chili oil
- 1 teaspoon ground Sichuan peppercorns (or black pepper)
- 2 garlic cloves, finely chopped
- 1 piece fresh ginger, peeled and finely chopped
- Kosher salt and freshly ground black pepper

Directions:
1. Insert the Crisper Basket and close the hood. Select ROAST, set the temperature to 375ºF, and set the time to 10 minutes. Select START/STOP to begin preheating.
2. Toss the broccoli florets with the chili oil, Sichuan peppercorns, garlic, ginger, salt, and pepper in a mixing bowl until thoroughly coated.
3. Transfer the broccoli florets to the Crisper Basket. Close the hood and ROAST for 10 minutes, shaking the basket halfway through, or until the broccoli florets are lightly browned and tender.
4. Remove the broccoli from the basket and serve on a plate.

Cauliflower Steaks With Ranch Dressing

Servings: 2 | Cooking Time: 15 Minutes

Ingredients:
- 1 head cauliflower, stemmed and leaves removed
- ¼ cup canola oil
- ½ teaspoon garlic powder
- ½ teaspoon paprika
- Sea salt, to taste
- Freshly ground black pepper, to taste
- 1 cup shredded Cheddar cheese
- Ranch dressing, for garnish
- 4 slices bacon, cooked and crumbled
- 2 tablespoons chopped fresh chives

Directions:
1. Cut the cauliflower from top to bottom into two 2-inch "steaks"; reserve the remaining cauliflower to cook separately.
2. Insert the Grill Grate and close the hood. Select GRILL, set the temperature to MAX, and set the time to 15 minutes. Select START/STOP to begin preheating.
3. Meanwhile, in a small bowl, whisk together the oil, garlic powder, and paprika. Season with salt and pepper. Brush each steak with the oil mixture on both sides.
4. When the unit beeps to signify it has preheated, place the steaks on the Grill Grate. Close the hood and GRILL for 10 minutes.
5. After 10 minutes, flip the steaks and top each with ½ cup of cheese. Close the hood and continue to GRILL until the cheese is melted, about 5 minutes.
6. When cooking is complete, place the cauliflower steaks on a plate and drizzle with the ranch dressing. Top with the bacon and chives.

Chermoula Beet Roast

Servings: 4 | Cooking Time: 25 Minutes

Ingredients:
- Chermoula:
- 1 cup packed fresh cilantro leaves
- ½ cup packed fresh parsley leaves
- 6 cloves garlic, peeled
- 2 teaspoons smoked paprika
- 2 teaspoons ground cumin
- 1 teaspoon ground coriander
- ½ to 1 teaspoon cayenne pepper
- Pinch of crushed saffron (optional)
- ½ cup extra-virgin olive oil
- Kosher salt, to taste
- Beets:
- 3 medium beets, trimmed, peeled, and cut into 1-inch chunks
- 2 tablespoons chopped fresh cilantro
- 2 tablespoons chopped fresh parsley

Directions:
1. In a food processor, combine the cilantro, parsley, garlic, paprika, cumin, coriander, and cayenne. Pulse until coarsely chopped. Add the saffron, if using, and process until combined. With the food processor running, slowly add the olive oil in a steady stream; process until the sauce is uniform. Season with salt.
2. Insert the Crisper Basket and close the hood. Select ROAST, set the temperature to 375°F, and set the time to 25 minutes. Select START/STOP to begin preheating.
3. In a large bowl, drizzle the beets with ½ cup of the chermoula to coat. Arrange the beets in the Crisper Basket. Close the hood and ROAST for 25 minutes, or until the beets are tender.
4. Transfer the beets to a serving platter. Sprinkle with the chopped cilantro and parsley and serve.

Black Bean And Tomato Chili

Servings: 6 | Cooking Time: 23 Minutes

Ingredients:
- 1 tablespoon olive oil
- 1 medium onion, diced
- 3 garlic cloves, minced
- 1 cup vegetable broth
- 3 cans black beans, drained and rinsed
- 2 cans diced tomatoes
- 2 chipotle peppers, chopped
- 2 teaspoons cumin
- 2 teaspoons chili powder
- 1 teaspoon dried oregano
- ½ teaspoon salt

Directions:
1. Over a medium heat, fry the garlic and onions in the olive oil for 3 minutes.
2. Add the remaining ingredients, stirring constantly and scraping the bottom to prevent sticking.
3. Select BAKE, set the temperature to 400°F, and set the time to 20 minutes. Select START/STOP to begin preheating.
4. Take a baking pan and place the mixture inside. Put a sheet of aluminum foil on top.
5. Place the pan directly in the pot. Close the hood and BAKE for 20 minutes.
6. When ready, plate up and serve immediately.

Balsamic Mushroom Sliders With Pesto

Servings: 4 | Cooking Time: 8 Minutes

Ingredients:
- 8 small portobello mushrooms, trimmed with gills removed
- 2 tablespoons canola oil
- 2 tablespoons balsamic vinegar
- 8 slider buns
- 1 tomato, sliced
- ½ cup pesto
- ½ cup micro greens

Directions:
1. Insert the Grill Grate and close the hood. Select GRILL, set the temperature to HIGH, and set the time to 8 minutes. Select START/STOP to begin preheating.
2. While the unit is preheating, brush the mushrooms with the oil and balsamic vinegar.
3. When the unit beeps to signify it has preheated, place the mushrooms, gill-side down, on the Grill Grate. Close the hood and GRILL for 8 minutes until the mushrooms are tender.
4. When cooking is complete, remove the mushrooms from the grill, and layer on the buns with tomato, pesto, and micro greens.

Honey-sriracha Brussels Sprouts

Servings: 8 | Cooking Time: 20 Minutes

Ingredients:
- 2 pounds Brussels sprouts, halved lengthwise, ends trimmed
- 2 tablespoons avocado oil
- 4 tablespoons honey or coconut palm sugar
- 2 teaspoons sriracha
- Juice of 1 lemon

Directions:
1. Insert the Crisper Basket and close the hood. Select AIR CRISP, set the temperature to 390°F, and set the time to 20 minutes. Select START/STOP to begin preheating.
2. While the unit is preheating, in a large bowl, toss the Brussels sprouts with the avocado oil.
3. When the unit beeps to signify it has preheated, place the Brussels sprouts in the Crisper Basket. Close the hood and cook for 10 minutes.
4. After 10 minutes, open the hood and toss the Brussels sprouts. Close the hood and cook for 10 minutes more. If you choose, before the last 5 minutes, open the hood and toss the Brussels sprouts one more time.
5. When cooking is complete, open the hood and transfer the Brussels sprouts to a large bowl. Or if you like more crisping and browning of your sprouts, continue cooking to your liking.
6. In a small bowl, whisk together the honey, sriracha, and lemon juice. Drizzle this over the Brussels sprouts and toss to coat. Serve.

Spicy Cauliflower Roast

Servings: 4 | Cooking Time: 20 Minutes

Ingredients:
- Cauliflower:
- 5 cups cauliflower florets
- 3 tablespoons vegetable oil
- ½ teaspoon ground cumin
- ½ teaspoon ground coriander
- ½ teaspoon kosher salt
- Sauce:
- ½ cup Greek yogurt or sour cream
- ¼ cup chopped fresh cilantro
- 1 jalapeño, coarsely chopped
- 4 cloves garlic, peeled
- ½ teaspoon kosher salt
- 2 tablespoons water

Directions:
1. Insert the Crisper Basket and close the hood. Select ROAST, set the temperature to 400°F, and set the time to 20 minutes. Select START/STOP to begin preheating.
2. In a large bowl, combine the cauliflower, oil, cumin, coriander, and salt. Toss to coat.
3. Put the cauliflower in the Crisper Basket. Close the hood and ROAST for 20 minutes, stirring halfway through the roasting time.
4. Meanwhile, in a blender, combine the yogurt, cilantro, jalapeño, garlic, and salt. Blend, adding the water as needed to keep the blades moving and to thin the sauce.
5. At the end of roasting time, transfer the cauliflower to a large serving bowl. Pour the sauce over and toss gently to coat. Serve immediately.

Corn Pakodas

Servings: 5 | Cooking Time: 8 Minutes

Ingredients:
- 1 cup flour
- ¼ teaspoon baking soda
- ¼ teaspoon salt
- ½ teaspoon curry powder
- ½ teaspoon red chili powder
- ¼ teaspoon turmeric powder
- ¼ cup water
- 10 cobs baby corn, blanched
- Cooking spray

Directions:
1. Insert the Crisper Basket and close the hood. Select AIR CRISP, set the temperature to 425°F, and set the time to 8 minutes. Select START/STOP to begin preheating.
2. Cover the Crisper Basket with aluminum foil and spritz with the cooking spray.
3. In a bowl, combine all the ingredients, save for the corn. Stir with a whisk until well combined.
4. Coat the corn in the batter and put inside the basket.
5. Close the hood and AIR CRISP for 8 minutes until a golden brown color is achieved.
6. Serve hot.

Crispy Noodle Vegetable Stir-fry

Servings: 4 | Cooking Time: 20 Minutes

Ingredients:

- 4 cups water
- 3 (5-ounce) packages instant ramen noodles (flavor packets removed) or 1 (12-ounce) package chow mein noodles
- Extra-virgin olive oil, for drizzling, plus 3 tablespoons
- 3 garlic cloves, minced
- 3 teaspoons peeled minced fresh ginger
- 1 red bell pepper, cut into thin strips
- 4 ounces white mushrooms, sliced
- 1 (8-ounce) can sweet baby corn, drained

- 2 cups snap peas
- 2 cups broccoli florets
- 1 small carrot, diagonally sliced
- 1 cup vegetable broth
- 1 cup soy sauce
- ¼ cup rice vinegar
- 1 tablespoon sesame oil
- 3 tablespoons sugar
- 1 tablespoon cornstarch

Directions:

1. Insert the Cooking Pot and close the hood. Select GRILL, set the temperature to HI, and set the time to 20 minutes. Select START/STOP to begin preheating.
2. When the unit beeps to signify it has preheated, pour the water into the Cooking Pot and add the ramen noodles. Close the hood and cook for 5 minutes.
3. After 5 minutes, open the hood and remove the Cooking Pot. Drain the noodles and set aside. Insert the Grill Grate (along with the Cooking Pot). Make a large bed of noodles on the Grill Grate and drizzle olive oil over them. Close the hood and cook for 5 minutes. (If using chow mein noodles, flip them halfway through.)
4. After 5 minutes, the ramen noodles should be crispy and golden brown. Transfer the crispy noodles to a large serving plate.
5. Use grill mitts to remove the Grill Grate. To the Cooking Pot, add the remaining 3 tablespoons of olive oil and the garlic and ginger. Close the hood and cook for 2 minutes.
6. After 2 minutes, open the hood and add the red bell pepper, mushrooms, baby corn, snap peas, broccoli, and carrot. Close the hood and cook for 5 minutes.
7. While the vegetables are cooking, in a small bowl, combine the vegetable broth, soy sauce, vinegar, sesame oil, sugar, and cornstarch and mix until the sugar and cornstarch are dissolved.
8. After 5 minutes, open the hood, stir the vegetables, and add the broth mixture. Close the hood and cook for 3 minutes more.
9. When cooking is complete, open the hood and stir once more. Close the hood and let the vegetables sit in the pot for 3 minutes. Then, pour the vegetables and sauce on top of the crispy noodle bed and serve.

Garlic Roasted Asparagus

Servings: 4 | Cooking Time: 10 Minutes

Ingredients:

- 1 pound asparagus, woody ends trimmed
- 2 tablespoons olive oil
- 1 tablespoon balsamic vinegar
- 2 teaspoons minced garlic
- Salt and freshly ground black pepper, to taste

Directions:

1. Insert the Crisper Basket and close the hood. Select ROAST, set the temperature to 400°F, and set the time to 10 minutes. Select START/STOP to begin preheating.
2. In a large shallow bowl, toss the asparagus with the olive oil, balsamic vinegar, garlic, salt, and pepper until thoroughly coated.
3. Arrange the asparagus in the Crisper Basket. Close the hood and ROAST for 10 minutes until crispy. Flip the asparagus with tongs halfway through the cooking time.
4. Serve warm.

Sriracha Golden Cauliflower

Servings: 4 | Cooking Time: 17 Minutes

Ingredients:
- ¼ cup vegan butter, melted
- ¼ cup sriracha sauce
- 4 cups cauliflower florets
- 1 cup bread crumbs
- 1 teaspoon salt

Directions:
1. Insert the Crisper Basket and close the hood. Select AIR CRISP, set the temperature to 375ºF, and set the time to 17 minutes. Select START/STOP to begin preheating.
2. Mix the sriracha and vegan butter in a bowl and pour this mixture over the cauliflower, taking care to cover each floret entirely.
3. In a separate bowl, combine the bread crumbs and salt.
4. Dip the cauliflower florets in the bread crumbs, coating each one well. Transfer to the basket. Close the hood and AIR CRISP for 17 minutes.
5. Serve hot.

Cheesy Broccoli Gratin

Servings: 2 | Cooking Time: 12 To 14 Minutes

Ingredients:
- ⅓ cup fat-free milk
- 1 tablespoon all-purpose or gluten-free flour
- ½ tablespoon olive oil
- ½ teaspoon ground sage
- ¼ teaspoon kosher salt
- ⅛ teaspoon freshly ground black pepper
- 2 cups roughly chopped broccoli florets
- 6 tablespoons shredded Cheddar cheese
- 2 tablespoons panko bread crumbs
- 1 tablespoon grated Parmesan cheese
- Olive oil spray

Directions:
1. Select BAKE, set the temperature to 330ºF, and set the time to 14 minutes. Select START/STOP to begin preheating.
2. Spritz a baking pan with olive oil spray.
3. Mix the milk, flour, olive oil, sage, salt, and pepper in a medium bowl and whisk to combine. Stir in the broccoli florets, Cheddar cheese, bread crumbs, and Parmesan cheese and toss to coat.
4. Pour the broccoli mixture into the prepared baking pan. Place the pan directly in the pot.
5. Close the hood and BAKE for 12 to 14 minutes until the top is golden brown and the broccoli is tender.
6. Serve immediately.

Creamy And Cheesy Spinach

Servings: 4 | Cooking Time: 15 Minutes

Ingredients:
- Vegetable oil spray
- 1 package frozen spinach, thawed and squeezed dry
- ½ cup chopped onion
- 2 cloves garlic, minced
- 4 ounces cream cheese, diced
- ½ teaspoon ground nutmeg
- 1 teaspoon kosher salt
- 1 teaspoon black pepper
- ½ cup grated Parmesan cheese

Directions:
1. Select BAKE, set the temperature to 350ºF, and set the time to 15 minutes. Select START/STOP to begin preheating.
2. Spray a heatproof pan with vegetable oil spray.
3. In a medium bowl, combine the spinach, onion, garlic, cream cheese, nutmeg, salt, and pepper. Transfer to the prepared pan.
4. Place the pan directly in the pot. Close the hood and BAKE for 10 minutes. Open and stir to thoroughly combine the cream cheese and spinach.
5. Sprinkle the Parmesan cheese on top. Bake for 5 minutes, or until the cheese has melted and browned.
6. Serve hot.

Summer Squash And Zucchini Salad

Servings: 4 | Cooking Time: 20 Minutes

Ingredients:
- 1 zucchini, sliced lengthwise about ¼-inch thick
- 1 summer squash, sliced lengthwise about ¼-inch thick
- ½ red onion, sliced
- 4 tablespoons canola oil, divided
- 2 portobello mushroom caps, trimmed with gills removed
- 2 ears corn, shucked
- 2 teaspoons freshly squeezed lemon juice
- Sea salt, to taste
- Freshly ground black pepper, to taste

Directions:
1. Insert the Grill Grate and close the hood. Select GRILL, set the temperature to MAX, and set the time to 25 minutes. Select START/STOP to begin preheating.
2. Meanwhile, in a large bowl, toss the zucchini, squash, and onion with 2 tablespoons of oil until evenly coated.
3. When the unit beeps to signify it has preheated, arrange the zucchini, squash, and onions on the Grill Grate. Close the hood and GRILL for 6 minutes.
4. After 6 minutes, open the hood and flip the squash. Close the hood and GRILL for 6 to 9 minutes more.
5. Meanwhile, brush the mushrooms and corn with the remaining 2 tablespoons of oil.
6. When cooking is complete, remove the zucchini, squash, and onions and swap in the mushrooms and corn. Close the hood and GRILL for the remaining 10 minutes.
7. When cooking is complete, remove the mushrooms and corn, and let cool.
8. Cut the kernels from the cobs. Roughly chop all the vegetables into bite-size pieces.
9. Place the vegetables in a serving bowl and drizzle with lemon juice. Season with salt and pepper, and toss until evenly mixed.

Buttered Broccoli With Parmesan

Servings: 4 | Cooking Time: 4 Minutes

Ingredients:
- 1 pound broccoli florets
- 1 medium shallot, minced
- 2 tablespoons olive oil
- 2 tablespoons unsalted butter, melted
- 2 teaspoons minced garlic
- ¼ cup grated Parmesan cheese

Directions:
1. Insert the Crisper Basket and close the hood. Select ROAST, set the temperature to 360°F, and set the time to 4 minutes. Select START/STOP to begin preheating.
2. Combine the broccoli florets with the shallot, olive oil, butter, garlic, and Parmesan cheese in a medium bowl and toss until the broccoli florets are thoroughly coated.
3. Arrange the broccoli florets in the Crisper Basket in a single layer. Close the hood and ROAST for 4 minutes until crisp-tender.
4. Serve warm.

Creamy Corn Casserole

Servings: 4 | Cooking Time: 15 Minutes

Ingredients:
- 2 cups frozen yellow corn
- 1 egg, beaten
- 3 tablespoons flour
- ½ cup grated Swiss or Havarti cheese
- ½ cup light cream
- ¼ cup milk
- Pinch salt
- Freshly ground black pepper, to taste
- 2 tablespoons butter, cut into cubes
- Nonstick cooking spray

Directions:
1. Select BAKE, set the temperature to 320°F, and set the time to 15 minutes. Select START/STOP to begin preheating.
2. Spritz a baking pan with nonstick cooking spray.
3. Stir together the remaining ingredients except the butter in a medium bowl until well incorporated.
4. Transfer the mixture to the prepared baking pan and scatter with the butter cubes.
5. Place the pan directly in the pot. Close the hood and BAKE for 15 minutes, or until the top is golden brown and a toothpick inserted in the center comes out clean.
6. Let the casserole cool for 5 minutes before slicing into wedges and serving.

Veggie Taco Pie

Servings: 4 | Cooking Time: 15 Minutes

Ingredients:
- 1 (15-ounce) can pinto beans, drained and rinsed
- 1 tablespoon chili powder
- 2 teaspoons ground cumin
- 2 teaspoons sea salt
- 1 teaspoon paprika
- ½ teaspoon garlic powder
- ½ teaspoon onion powder
- ½ teaspoon dried oregano
- 4 small flour tortillas
- 1 cup sour cream
- 1 (14-ounce) can diced tomatoes, drained
- 1 (15-ounce) can black beans, drained and rinsed
- 2 cups shredded cheddar cheese

Directions:
1. Insert the Cooking Pot and close the hood. Select BAKE, set the temperature to 350°F, and set the time to 15 minutes. Select START/STOP to begin preheating.
2. While the unit is preheating, in a large bowl, mash the pinto beans with a fork. Add the chili powder, cumin, salt, paprika, garlic powder, onion powder, and oregano and mix until well combined. Place a tortilla in the bottom of a 6-inch springform pan. Spread a quarter of the mashed pinto beans on the tortilla in an even layer, then layer on a quarter each of the sour cream, tomatoes, black beans, and cheddar cheese in that order. Repeat the layers three more times, ending with cheese.
3. When the unit beeps to signify it has preheated, place the pan in the Cooking Pot. Close the hood and cook for 15 minutes.
4. When cooking is complete, the cheese will be melted. Remove the pan from the grill and serve.

Grilled Vegetable Pizza

Servings: 2 | Cooking Time: 10 Minutes

Ingredients:
- 2 tablespoons all-purpose flour, plus more as needed
- ½ store-bought pizza dough
- 1 tablespoon canola oil, divided
- ½ cup pizza sauce
- 1 cup shredded Mozzarella cheese
- ½ zucchini, thinly sliced
- ½ red onion, sliced
- ½ red bell pepper, seeded and thinly sliced

Directions:
1. Insert the Grill Grate and close the hood. Select GRILL, set the temperature to MAX, and set the time to 7 minutes. Select START/STOP to begin preheating.
2. While the unit is preheating, dust a clean work surface with the flour.
3. Place the dough on the floured surface and roll it into a 9-inch round of even thickness. Dust your rolling pin and work surface with additional flour, as needed, to ensure the dough does not stick.
4. Evenly brush the surface of the rolled-out dough with ½ tablespoon of oil. Flip the dough over and brush the other side with the remaining ½ tablespoon of oil. Poke the dough with a fork 5 or 6 times across its surface to prevent air pockets from forming while it cooks.
5. When the unit beeps to signify it has preheated, place the dough on the Grill Grate. Close the hood and GRILL for 4 minutes.
6. After 4 minutes, flip the dough, then spread the pizza sauce evenly over it. Sprinkle with the cheese, and top with the zucchini, onion, and pepper.
7. Close the hood and continue cooking for the remaining 2 to 3 minutes until the cheese is melted and the veggie slices begin to crisp.
8. When cooking is complete, let cool slightly before slicing.

Honey-glazed Roasted Veggies

Servings:3 | Cooking Time: 20 Minutes

Ingredients:
- Glaze:
- 2 tablespoons raw honey
- 2 teaspoons minced garlic
- ¼ teaspoon dried marjoram
- ¼ teaspoon dried basil
- ¼ teaspoon dried oregano
- ⅛ teaspoon dried sage
- ⅛ teaspoon dried rosemary
- ⅛ teaspoon dried thyme
- ½ teaspoon salt
- ¼ teaspoon ground black pepper
- Veggies:
- 3 to 4 medium red potatoes, cut into 1- to 2-inch pieces
- 1 small zucchini, cut into 1- to 2-inch pieces
- 1 small carrot, sliced into ¼-inch rounds
- 1 package cherry tomatoes, halved
- 1 cup sliced mushrooms
- 3 tablespoons olive oil

Directions:
1. Insert the Crisper Basket and close the hood. Select ROAST, set the temperature to 380ºF, and set the time to 15 minutes. Select START/STOP to begin preheating.
2. Combine the honey, garlic, marjoram, basil, oregano, sage, rosemary, thyme, salt, and pepper in a small bowl and stir to mix well. Set aside.
3. Place the red potatoes, zucchini, carrot, cherry tomatoes, and mushroom in a large bowl. Drizzle with the olive oil and toss to coat.
4. Pour the veggies into the Crisper Basket. Close the hood and ROAST for 15 minutes, shaking the basket halfway through.
5. When ready, transfer the roasted veggies to the large bowl. Pour the honey mixture over the veggies, tossing to coat.
6. Spread out the veggies in a baking pan and place in the grill.
7. Increase the temperature to 390ºF and ROAST for an additional 5 minutes, or until the veggies are tender and glazed. Serve warm.

Mozzarella Broccoli Calzones

Servings: 4 | Cooking Time: 24 Minutes

Ingredients:

- 1 head broccoli, trimmed into florets
- 2 tablespoons extra-virgin olive oil
- 1 store-bought pizza dough
- 2 to 3 tablespoons all-purpose flour, plus more for dusting
- 1 egg, beaten
- 2 cups shredded Mozzarella cheese
- 1 cup ricotta cheese
- ½ cup grated Parmesan cheese
- 1 garlic clove, grated
- Grated zest of 1 lemon
- ½ teaspoon red pepper flakes
- Cooking oil spray

Directions:

1. Insert the Crisper Basket and close the hood. Select AIR CRISP, set the temperature to 390°F, and set the time to 12 minutes. Select START/STOP to begin preheating.
2. Meanwhile, in a large bowl, toss the broccoli and olive oil until evenly coated.
3. When the unit beeps to signify it has preheated, add the broccoli to the basket. Close the hood and AIR CRISP for 6 minutes.
4. While the broccoli is cooking, divide the pizza dough into four equal pieces. Dust a clean work surface with the flour. Place the dough on the floured surface and roll each piece into an 8-inch round of even thickness. Dust your rolling pin and work surface with additional flour, as needed, to ensure the dough does not stick. Brush a thin coating of egg wash around the edges of each round.
5. After 6 minutes, shake the basket of broccoli. Place the basket back in the unit and close the hood to resume cooking.
6. Meanwhile, in a medium bowl, combine the Mozzarella, ricotta, Parmesan cheese, garlic, lemon zest, and red pepper flakes.
7. After cooking is complete, add the broccoli to the cheese mixture. Spoon one-quarter of the mixture onto one side of each dough. Fold the other half over the filling, and press firmly to seal the edges together. Brush each calzone all over with the remaining egg wash.
8. Select AIR CRISP, set the temperature to 390°F, and set the time to 12 minutes. Select START/STOP to begin preheating.
9. When the unit beeps to signify it has preheated, coat the Crisper Basket with cooking spray and place the calzones in the basket. AIR CRISP for 10 to 12 minutes, until golden brown.

Prosciutto Mini Mushroom Pizza

Servings: 3 | Cooking Time: 5 Minutes

Ingredients:

- 3 portobello mushroom caps, cleaned and scooped
- 3 tablespoons olive oil
- Pinch of salt
- Pinch of dried Italian seasonings
- 3 tablespoons tomato sauce
- 3 tablespoons shredded Mozzarella cheese
- 12 slices prosciutto

Directions:

1. Insert the Crisper Basket and close the hood. Select AIR CRISP, set the temperature to 330°F, and set the time to 5 minutes. Select START/STOP to begin preheating.
2. Season both sides of the portobello mushrooms with a drizzle of olive oil, then sprinkle salt and the Italian seasonings on the insides.
3. With a knife, spread the tomato sauce evenly over the mushroom, before adding the Mozzarella on top.
4. Put the portobello in the Crisper Basket. Close the hood and AIR CRISP for 1 minutes, before taking the Crisper Basket out of the grill and putting the prosciutto slices on top. AIR CRISP for another 4 minutes.
5. Serve warm.

Green Beans With Sun-dried Tomatoes And Feta

Servings: 8 | Cooking Time: 8 Minutes

Ingredients:
- 2 pounds green beans, ends trimmed
- 2 tablespoons extra-virgin olive oil
- 1 teaspoon salt
- ½ teaspoon freshly ground black pepper
- 1 cup sun-dried tomatoes packed in oil, undrained, sliced
- 6 ounces feta cheese, crumbled

Directions:
1. Insert the Grill Grate and close the hood. Select GRILL, set the temperature to HI, and set the time to 8 minutes. Select START/STOP to begin preheating.
2. While the unit is preheating, in a large bowl, toss the green beans with the olive oil, salt, and pepper.
3. When the unit beeps to signify it has preheated, place the green beans on the Grill Grate. Close the hood and grill for 4 minutes.
4. After 4 minutes, open the hood and flip the green beans. Close the hood and cook for 4 minutes more.
5. When cooking is complete, transfer the green beans to a large bowl. Add the sun-dried tomatoes and mix together. Top with the feta cheese and serve.

Rosemary Roasted Squash With Cheese

Servings: 2 | Cooking Time: 20 Minutes

Ingredients:
- 1 pound butternut squash, cut into wedges
- 2 tablespoons olive oil
- 1 tablespoon dried rosemary
- Salt, to salt
- 1 cup crumbled goat cheese
- 1 tablespoon maple syrup

Directions:
1. Insert the Crisper Basket and close the hood. Select ROAST, set the temperature to 350°F, and set the time to 20 minutes. Select START/STOP to begin preheating.
2. Toss the squash wedges with the olive oil, rosemary, and salt in a large bowl until well coated.
3. Transfer the squash wedges to the Crisper Basket, spreading them out in as even a layer as possible.
4. Close the hood and ROAST for 10 minutes. Flip the squash and roast for another 10 minutes until golden brown.
5. Sprinkle the goat cheese on top and serve drizzled with the maple syrup.

Black-pepper Garlic Tofu

Servings: 4 | Cooking Time: 9 Minutes

Ingredients:

- 1 (14-ounce) package firm tofu, cut into 1-inch cubes
- 1½ teaspoons cornstarch, divided
- 2 tablespoons avocado oil
- 1 medium white onion, diced
- 1 red bell pepper, cut into thin strips
- 1 teaspoon peeled minced fresh ginger
- 2 garlic cloves, minced
- 2 tablespoons black peppercorns, crushed
- 2 tablespoons soy sauce
- 1 tablespoon light brown sugar, packed
- ¼ cup ketchup
- 1 tablespoon unsalted butter, melted

Directions:

1. Insert the Cooking Pot and close the hood. Select GRILL, set the temperature to MED, and set the time to 9 minutes. Select START/STOP to begin preheating.
2. While the unit is preheating, on a large plate, coat the tofu cubes with 1 teaspoon of cornstarch.
3. When the unit beeps to signify it has preheated, add the avocado oil to the Cooking Pot. Then add the tofu and stir with a wooden spoon. Close the hood and cook for 3 minutes.
4. After 3 minutes, open the hood and flip and mix the tofu around. Add the onion, red bell pepper, ginger, and garlic. Stir to mix well. Close the hood and cook for 3 minutes.
5. While the tofu is cooking, in a small bowl, mix together the black peppercorns, soy sauce, brown sugar, ketchup, butter, and remaining ½ teaspoon of cornstarch until the sugar and cornstarch are dissolved.
6. After 3 minutes, open the hood. Pour in the sauce and stir. Close the hood and cook for 3 minutes more.
7. When cooking is complete, open the hood and stir the mixture one more time. Serve.

Double "egg" Plant (eggplant Omelets)

Servings: 4 | Cooking Time: 16 Minutes

Ingredients:

- 4 Chinese eggplants
- 2 large eggs
- Garlic powder
- Salt
- Freshly ground black pepper
- ¼ cup ketchup
- 1 tablespoon hot sauce (optional)

Directions:

1. Insert the Grill Grate. Select GRILL, set the temperature to HI, and set the time to 10 minutes. Select START/STOP to begin preheating.
2. When the unit beeps to signify it has preheated, place the whole eggplants on the Grill Grate. Close the hood and cook for 5 minutes.
3. After 5 minutes, open the hood and flip the eggplants. Close the hood and cook for 5 minutes more.
4. When cooking is complete, the eggplant skin will be charred and cracked and the flesh will be soft. Remove the eggplants from the grill and set aside to cool.
5. Once the eggplants have cooled down, peel the skin. Then, using a fork, flatten the eggplants with a brushing motion until they become pear shaped and about the thickness of a pancake.
6. Select GRILL, set the temperature to HI, and set the time to 6 minutes. Select START/STOP to begin preheating.
7. While the unit is preheating, in a large bowl, whisk the eggs. Dip each eggplant into the egg mixture to coat both sides, then season both sides with garlic powder, salt, and pepper.
8. When the grill beeps to signify it has preheated, place the coated eggplants on the Grill Grate. Close the hood and grill for 3 minutes.
9. After 3 minutes, open the hood and flip the eggplants. Close the hood and cook for 3 minutes more. Add more time if needed until you get your desired crispiness of the omelets.
10. When cooking is complete, remove the eggplant omelets from the grill. In a small bowl, combine the ketchup and hot sauce (if using), or just use ketchup if you do not like spice, and serve alongside the omelets for dipping.

Simple Ratatouille

Servings: 2 | Cooking Time: 16 Minutes

Ingredients:
- 2 Roma tomatoes, thinly sliced
- 1 zucchini, thinly sliced
- 2 yellow bell peppers, sliced
- 2 garlic cloves, minced
- 2 tablespoons olive oil
- 2 tablespoons herbes de Provence
- 1 tablespoon vinegar
- Salt and black pepper, to taste

Directions:
1. Select ROAST, set the temperature to 390°F, and set the time to 16 minutes. Select START/STOP to begin preheating.
2. Place the tomatoes, zucchini, bell peppers, garlic, olive oil, herbes de Provence, and vinegar in a large bowl and toss until the vegetables are evenly coated. Sprinkle with salt and pepper and toss again. Pour the vegetable mixture into the pot.
3. Close the hood and ROAST for 8 minutes. Stir and continue roasting for 8 minutes until tender.
4. Let the vegetable mixture stand for 5 minutes in the basket before removing and serving.

Spicy Cabbage

Servings: 4 | Cooking Time: 7 Minutes

Ingredients:
- 1 head cabbage, sliced into 1-inch-thick ribbons
- 1 tablespoon olive oil
- 1 teaspoon garlic powder
- 1 teaspoon red pepper flakes
- 1 teaspoon salt
- 1 teaspoon freshly ground black pepper

Directions:
1. Insert the Crisper Basket and close the hood. Select ROAST, set the temperature to 350°F, and set the time to 7 minutes. Select START/STOP to begin preheating.
2. Toss the cabbage with the olive oil, garlic powder, red pepper flakes, salt, and pepper in a large mixing bowl until well coated.
3. Arrange the cabbage in the Crisper Basket. Close the hood and ROAST for 7 minutes until crisp. Flip the cabbage with tongs halfway through the cooking time.
4. Remove from the basket to a plate and serve warm.

Sides, Snacks & Appetizers

One-pot Nachos

Servings: 4 | Cooking Time: 10 Minutes

Ingredients:
- 1 pound ground beef
- 1 (1-ounce) packet taco seasoning mix
- 1 (16-ounce) can refried beans
- 1 (14.5-ounce) can diced tomatoes, drained
- 2 cups sour cream
- 3 cups shredded Mexican cheese blend
- 2 cups shredded iceberg lettuce
- 1 cup sliced black olives
- Sliced scallions, both white and green parts, for garnish
- 1 (10- to 13-ounce) bag tortilla chips

Directions:
1. Insert the Cooking Pot and close the hood. Select GRILL, set the temperature to MED, and set the time to 10 minutes. Select START/STOP to begin preheating.
2. When the unit beeps to signify it has preheated, place the ground beef in the Cooking Pot and sprinkle it with the taco seasoning. Using a wooden spoon or spatula, break apart the ground beef. Close the hood and cook for 5 minutes.
3. After 5 minutes, open the hood and stir the ground beef to mix a little more with the taco seasoning. Evenly spread the ground beef across the bottom of the pot. Add the refried beans in an even layer over the meat, then an even layer of the diced tomatoes. Close the hood and cook for 5 minutes more.
4. When cooking is complete, remove the Cooking Pot from the unit and place it on a heatproof surface. Add an even layer each of sour cream, shredded cheese, shredded lettuce, and olives on top. Garnish with scallions and serve with the tortilla chips.

Crispy Prosciutto-wrapped Asparagus

Servings: 6 | Cooking Time: 16 To 24 Minutes

Ingredients:
- 12 asparagus spears, woody ends trimmed
- 24 pieces thinly sliced prosciutto
- Cooking spray

Directions:
1. Insert the Crisper Basket and close the hood. Select AIR CRISP, set the temperature to 360°F, and set the time to 4 minutes. Select START/STOP to begin preheating.
2. Wrap each asparagus spear with 2 slices of prosciutto, then repeat this process with the remaining asparagus and prosciutto.
3. Spray the Crisper Basket with cooking spray, then place 2 to 3 bundles in the basket. Close the hood and AIR CRISP for 4 minutes. Repeat this process with the remaining asparagus bundles.
4. Remove the bundles and allow to cool on a wire rack for 5 minutes before serving.

Garlic Fries

Servings: 4 | Cooking Time: 20 Minutes

Ingredients:
- 2 large Idaho or russet potatoes (1½ to 2 pounds)
- 1 head garlic (10 to 12 cloves)
- 4 tablespoons avocado oil, divided
- 1 teaspoon sea salt
- Chopped fresh parsley, for garnish

Directions:
1. Cut the potatoes into ¼-inch-thick slices. Place the slices in a large bowl and cover with cold water. Set aside for 30 minutes. This will ensure the potatoes cook well and crisp up perfectly. While the potatoes are soaking, mince the garlic cloves.
2. Drain the potatoes and pat dry using paper towels. In a large bowl, toss the potato slices with 2 tablespoons of avocado oil.
3. Insert the Cooking Pot and Crisper Basket and close the hood. Select AIR CRISP, set the temperature to 390°F, and set the time to 20 minutes. Select START/STOP to begin preheating.
4. While the unit is preheating, in a small bowl, combine the remaining 2 tablespoons of avocado oil with the minced garlic.
5. When the unit beeps to signify it has preheated, put the fries in the Crisper Basket. Close the hood and cook for 10 minutes.
6. After 10 minutes, open the hood and give the basket a shake to toss the fries. Close the hood and continue cooking for 5 minutes. Open the hood again and give the basket a shake. Close the hood and cook for 5 minutes more.
7. When cooking is complete, the fries will be crispy and golden brown. If you like them extra-crispy, continue cooking to your liking. Transfer the fries to a large bowl and drizzle with the garlic oil. Toss and season with the salt. Garnish with the parsley and serve.

Bacon-wrapped Onion Rings And Spicy Aioli

Servings: 4 | Cooking Time: 10 Minutes

Ingredients:
- For the onion rings
- 3 large white onions
- 2 (1-pound) packages thin-sliced bacon
- For the spicy garlic aioli sauce
- 1 cup mayonnaise
- ¼ teaspoon garlic powder
- 1 tablespoon sriracha
- 1 teaspoon freshly squeezed lemon juice

Directions:
1. Insert the Grill Grate and close the hood. Select GRILL, set the temperature to MED, and set the time to 10 minutes. Select START/STOP to begin preheating.
2. While the unit is preheating, cut both ends off the onions. Slice each onion crosswise into thirds and peel off the outer layer of onion skin. Separate the onion rings, keeping two onion layers together to have a stable and firm ring. Wrap each onion ring pair with a slice of bacon. The bacon should slightly overlap itself as you wrap it all the way around the onion ring. Larger rings may need 2 slices of bacon.
3. When the unit beeps to signify it has preheated, place the onion rings on the Grill Grate. Close the hood and grill for 10 minutes. Flipping is not necessary.
4. When cooking is complete, the bacon will be cooked through and starting to crisp. If you prefer the bacon crispier or even close to charred, continue cooking to your liking.
5. While the onion rings are cooking, in a small bowl, whisk together the mayonnaise, garlic powder, sriracha, and lemon juice. Use more or less sriracha depending on your preferred spice level. Serve with the bacon onion rings.

Avocado Egg Rolls

Servings: 4 | Cooking Time: 10 Minutes

Ingredients:
- 4 avocados, pitted and diced
- ½ white onion, diced
- ⅓ cup sun-dried tomatoes, chopped
- 1 (16-ounce) package egg roll wrappers (about 20 wrappers)
- ¼ cup water, for sealing
- 4 tablespoons avocado oil

Directions:
1. Insert the Grill Grate and close the hood. Select GRILL, set the temperature to LO, and set the time to 10 minutes. Select START/STOP to begin preheating.
2. While the unit is preheating, place the diced avocado in a large bowl. Add the onion and sun-dried tomatoes and gently fold together, being careful to not mash the avocado.
3. Place an egg roll wrapper on a flat surface with a corner facing you (like a diamond). Add 2 to 3 tablespoons of the filling in the center of the wrapper. The amount should be about 2½ inches wide. Gently lift the bottom corner of the wrapper over the filling, fold in the sides, and roll away from you to close. Dip your finger into the water and run it over the top corner of the wrapper to seal it. Continue filling, folding, and sealing the rest of the egg rolls.
4. When the unit beeps to signify it has preheated, brush the avocado oil on all sides of the egg rolls. Place the egg rolls on the Grill Grate, seam-side down. Close the hood and grill for 5 minutes.
5. After 5 minutes, open the hood and flip the egg rolls. Give them another brush of avocado oil. Close the hood and cook for 5 minutes more.
6. When cooking is complete, the wrappers will be golden brown. Remove from the grill and serve.

Breaded Green Olives

Servings: 4 | Cooking Time: 8 Minutes

Ingredients:
- 1 jar pitted green olives
- ½ cup all-purpose flour
- Salt and pepper, to taste
- ½ cup bread crumbs
- 1 egg
- Cooking spray

Directions:
1. Insert the Crisper Basket and close the hood. Select AIR CRISP, set the temperature to 400°F, and set the time to 8 minutes. Select START/STOP to begin preheating.
2. Remove the olives from the jar and dry thoroughly with paper towels.
3. In a small bowl, combine the flour with salt and pepper to taste. Place the bread crumbs in another small bowl. In a third small bowl, beat the egg.
4. Spritz the Crisper Basket with cooking spray.
5. Dip the olives in the flour, then the egg, and then the bread crumbs.
6. Place the breaded olives in the basket. It is okay to stack them. Spray the olives with cooking spray. Close the hood and AIR CRISP for 6 minutes. Flip the olives and AIR CRISP for an additional 2 minutes, or until brown and crisp.
7. Cool before serving.

Deluxe Cheese Sandwiches

Servings: 4 To 8 | Cooking Time: 5 To 6 Minutes

Ingredients:
- 8 ounces Brie
- 8 slices oat nut bread
- 1 large ripe pear, cored and cut into ½-inch-thick slices
- 2 tablespoons butter, melted

Directions:
1. Select BAKE, set the temperature to 360ºF, and set the time to 6 minutes. Select START/STOP to begin preheating. .
2. Make the sandwiches: Spread each of 4 slices of bread with ¼ of the Brie. Top the Brie with the pear slices and remaining 4 bread slices.
3. Brush the melted butter lightly on both sides of each sandwich.
4. Arrange the sandwiches in a baking pan. You may need to work in batches to avoid overcrowding.
5. Place the pan directly in the pot. Close the hood and BAKE for 5 to 6 minutes until the cheese is melted. Repeat with the remaining sandwiches.
6. Serve warm.

Roasted Mixed Nuts

Servings: 6 | Cooking Time: 20 Minutes

Ingredients:
- 2 cups mixed nuts (walnuts, pecans, and almonds)
- 2 tablespoons egg white
- 2 tablespoons sugar
- 1 teaspoon paprika
- 1 teaspoon ground cinnamon
- Cooking spray

Directions:
1. Spray the Crisper Basket with cooking spray.
2. Insert the Crisper Basket and close the hood. Select ROAST, set the temperature to 300ºF, and set the time to 20 minutes. Select START/STOP to begin preheating.
3. Stir together the mixed nuts, egg white, sugar, paprika, and cinnamon in a small bowl until the nuts are fully coated.
4. Put the nuts in the Crisper Basket. Close the hood and ROAST for 20 minutes. Shake the basket halfway through the cooking time for even cooking.
5. Transfer the nuts to a bowl and serve warm.

Queso Bomb

Servings: 6 | Cooking Time: 15 Minutes

Ingredients:
- 1 (1-pound) block easy-melt cheese
- 1 pound ground country breakfast sausage (not links)
- 2 tablespoons minced garlic
- 2 cups shredded Mexican cheese blend or three-cheese blend
- 1 (10-ounce) can diced tomatoes with green chiles
- 1 (10- to 13-ounce) bag tortilla chips

Directions:
1. Insert the Cooking Pot and close the hood. Select GRILL, set the temperature to MED, and set the time to 15 minutes. Select START/STOP to begin preheating.
2. While the unit is preheating, slice the cheese block into 3-inch sections.
3. When the unit beeps to signify it has preheated, place the sausage and garlic in the Cooking Pot. Using a wooden spoon or spatula, break the sausage apart. Close the hood and cook for 5 minutes.
4. After 5 minutes, open the hood and stir the sausage. Add the pieces of easy-melt cheese, then add the shredded cheese blend in an even layer. Pour the diced tomatoes and green chiles with their juices into the pot. Close the hood and cook for 5 minutes.
5. After 5 minutes, stir the sausage and cheese together. Close the hood and cook 5 minutes more.
6. When cooking is complete, the cheese will be fully melted. Serve warm with tortilla chips.

Buttermilk Marinated Chicken Wings

Servings: 4 | Cooking Time: 17 To 19 Minutes

Ingredients:

- 2 pounds chicken wings
- Marinade:
- 1 cup buttermilk
- ½ teaspoon salt
- ½ teaspoon black pepper
- Coating:

- 1 cup flour
- 1 cup panko bread crumbs
- 2 tablespoons poultry seasoning
- 2 teaspoons salt
- Cooking spray

Directions:

1. Whisk together all the ingredients for the marinade in a large bowl.
2. Add the chicken wings to the marinade and toss well. Transfer to the refrigerator to marinate for at least an hour.
3. Spritz the Crisper Basket with cooking spray.
4. Insert the Crisper Basket and close the hood. Select AIR CRISP, set the temperature to 360ºF, and set the time to 19 minutes. Select START/STOP to begin preheating.
5. Thoroughly combine all the ingredients for the coating in a shallow bowl.
6. Remove the chicken wings from the marinade and shake off any excess. Roll them in the coating mixture.
7. Place the chicken wings in the Crisper Basket in a single layer. Mist the wings with cooking spray. You'll need to work in batches to avoid overcrowding.
8. Close the hood and AIR CRISP for 17 to 19 minutes, or until the wings are crisp and golden brown on the outside. Flip the wings halfway through the cooking time.
9. Remove from the basket to a plate and repeat with the remaining wings.
10. Serve hot.

Sweet Potato Chips

Servings:1 | Cooking Time: 8 To 10 Hours

Ingredients:

- 1 sweet potato, peeled
- ½ tablespoon avocado oil
- ½ teaspoon sea salt

Directions:

1. Using a mandoline, thinly slice (⅛ inch or less) the sweet potato.
2. In a large bowl, toss the sweet potato slices with the oil until evenly coated. Season with the salt.
3. Place the sweet potato slices flat on the Crisper Basket. Arrange them in a single layer, without any slices touching each another.
4. Place the basket in the pot and close the hood.
5. Select DEHYDRATE, set the temperature to 120ºF, and set the time to 10 hours. Select START/STOP.
6. After 8 hours, check for desired doneness. Continue dehydrating for 2 more hours, if necessary.
7. When cooking is complete, remove the basket from the pot. Transfer the sweet potato chips to an airtight container and store at room temperature.

Cheesy Summer Squash With Red Onion

Servings: 4 | Cooking Time: 15 Minutes

Ingredients:
- ½ cup vegetable oil, plus 3 tablespoons
- ¼ cup white wine vinegar
- 1 garlic clove, grated
- 2 summer squash, sliced lengthwise about ¼-inch thick
- 1 red onion, peeled and cut into wedges
- Sea salt, to taste
- Freshly ground black pepper, to taste
- 1 package crumbled feta cheese
- Red pepper flakes, as needed

Directions:
1. Insert the Grill Grate and close the hood. Select GRILL, set the temperature to MAX, and set the time to 15 minutes. Select START/STOP to begin preheating.
2. Meanwhile, in a small bowl, whisk together ½ cup oil, vinegar, and garlic, and set aside.
3. In a large bowl, toss the squash and onion with remaining 3 tablespoons of oil until evenly coated. Season with the salt and pepper.
4. When the unit beeps to signify it has preheated, arrange the squash and onions on the Grill Grate. Close the hood and GRILL for 6 minutes.
5. After 6 minutes, open the hood and flip the squash. Close the hood and GRILL for 6 to 9 minutes more.
6. When vegetables are cooked to desired doneness, remove them from the grill. Arrange the vegetables on a large platter and top with the feta cheese. Drizzle the dressing over the top, and sprinkle with the red pepper flakes. Let stand for 15 minutes before serving.

Rosemary Baked Cashews

Servings:2 | Cooking Time: 3 Minutes

Ingredients:
- 2 sprigs of fresh rosemary
- 1 teaspoon olive oil
- 1 teaspoon kosher salt
- ½ teaspoon honey
- 2 cups roasted and unsalted whole cashews
- Cooking spray

Directions:
1. Insert the Crisper Basket and close the hood. Select BAKE, set the temperature to 300ºF, and set the time to 3 minutes. Select START/STOP to begin preheating.
2. In a medium bowl, whisk together the chopped rosemary, olive oil, kosher salt, and honey. Set aside.
3. Spray the Crisper Basket with cooking spray, then place the cashews and the whole rosemary sprig in the basket. Close the hood and BAKE for 3 minutes.
4. Remove the cashews and rosemary from the grill, then discard the rosemary and add the cashews to the olive oil mixture, tossing to coat.
5. Allow to cool for 15 minutes before serving.

Spicy Kale Chips

Servings: 4 | Cooking Time: 8 To 12 Minutes

Ingredients:
- 5 cups kale, large stems removed and chopped
- 2 teaspoons canola oil
- ¼ teaspoon smoked paprika
- ¼ teaspoon kosher salt
- Cooking spray

Directions:
1. Insert the Crisper Basket and close the hood. Select AIR CRISP, set the temperature to 390ºF, and set the time to 6 minutes. Select START/STOP to begin preheating.
2. In a large bowl, toss the kale, canola oil, smoked paprika, and kosher salt.
3. Spray the Crisper Basket with cooking spray, then place half the kale in the basket. Close the hood and AIR CRISP for 2 to 3 minutes.
4. Shake the basket and AIR CRISP for 2 to 3 more minutes, or until crispy. Repeat this process with the remaining kale.
5. Remove the kale and allow to cool on a wire rack for 3 to 5 minutes before serving.

Crispy Cod Fingers

Servings: 4 | Cooking Time: 12 Minutes

Ingredients:
- 2 eggs
- 2 tablespoons milk
- 2 cups flour
- 1 cup cornmeal
- 1 teaspoon seafood seasoning
- Salt and black pepper, to taste
- 1 cup bread crumbs
- 1 pound cod fillets, cut into 1-inch strips

Directions:
1. Insert the Crisper Basket and close the hood. Select AIR CRISP, set the temperature to 400°F, and set the time to 12 minutes. Select START/STOP to begin preheating.
2. Beat the eggs with the milk in a shallow bowl. In another shallow bowl, combine the flour, cornmeal, seafood seasoning, salt, and pepper. On a plate, place the bread crumbs.
3. Dredge the cod strips, one at a time, in the flour mixture, then in the egg mixture, finally in the bread crumb to coat evenly.
4. Arrange the cod strips in the Crisper Basket. Close the hood and AIR CRISP for 12 minutes until crispy.
5. Transfer the cod strips to a paper towel-lined plate and serve warm.

Caramelized Peaches

Servings: 4 | Cooking Time: 10 To 13 Minutes

Ingredients:
- 2 tablespoons sugar
- ¼ teaspoon ground cinnamon
- 4 peaches, cut into wedges
- Cooking spray

Directions:
1. Lightly spray the Crisper Basket with cooking spray.
2. Insert the Crisper Basket and close the hood. Select AIR CRISP, set the temperature to 350°F, and set the time to 13 minutes. Select START/STOP to begin preheating.
3. Toss the peaches with the sugar and cinnamon in a medium bowl until evenly coated.
4. Arrange the peaches in the Crisper Basket in a single layer. Lightly mist the peaches with cooking spray. You may need to work in batches to avoid overcrowding.
5. Close the hood and AIR CRISP for 5 minutes. Flip the peaches and AIR CRISP for another 5 to 8 minutes, or until the peaches are caramelized.
6. Repeat with the remaining peaches.
7. Let the peaches cool for 5 minutes and serve warm.

Breaded Artichoke Hearts

Servings: 14 | Cooking Time: 8 Minutes

Ingredients:
- 14 whole artichoke hearts, packed in water
- 1 egg
- ½ cup all-purpose flour
- ⅓ cup panko bread crumbs
- 1 teaspoon Italian seasoning
- Cooking spray

Directions:
1. Insert the Crisper Basket and close the hood. Select AIR CRISP, set the temperature to 380°F, and set the time to 8 minutes. Select START/STOP to begin preheating.
2. Squeeze excess water from the artichoke hearts and place them on paper towels to dry.
3. In a small bowl, beat the egg. In another small bowl, place the flour. In a third small bowl, combine the bread crumbs and Italian seasoning, and stir.
4. Spritz the Crisper Basket with cooking spray.
5. Dip the artichoke hearts in the flour, then the egg, and then the bread crumb mixture.
6. Place the breaded artichoke hearts in the Crisper Basket. Spray them with cooking spray.
7. Close the hood and AIR CRISP for 8 minutes, or until the artichoke hearts have browned and are crisp, flipping once halfway through.
8. Let cool for 5 minutes before serving.

Herbed Pita Chips

Servings: 4 | Cooking Time: 5 To 6 Minutes

Ingredients:
- ¼ teaspoon dried basil
- ¼ teaspoon marjoram
- ¼ teaspoon ground oregano
- ¼ teaspoon garlic powder
- ¼ teaspoon ground thyme
- ¼ teaspoon salt
- 2 whole 6-inch pitas, whole grain or white
- Cooking spray

Directions:
1. Insert the Crisper Basket and close the hood. Select BAKE, set the temperature to 330°F, and set the time to 6 minutes. Select START/STOP to begin preheating.
2. Mix all the seasonings together.
3. Cut each pita half into 4 wedges. Break apart wedges at the fold.
4. Mist one side of pita wedges with oil. Sprinkle with half of seasoning mix.
5. Turn pita wedges over, mist the other side with oil, and sprinkle with remaining seasonings.
6. Place pita wedges in Crisper Basket. Close the hood and BAKE for 2 minutes.
7. Shake the basket and bake for 2 minutes longer. Shake again, and if needed, bake for 1 or 2 more minutes, or until crisp. Watch carefully because at this point they will cook very quickly.
8. Serve hot.

Cheesy Apple Roll-ups

Servings:8 | Cooking Time: 4 To 5 Minutes

Ingredients:
- 8 slices whole wheat sandwich bread
- 4 ounces Colby Jack cheese, grated
- ½ small apple, chopped
- 2 tablespoons butter, melted

Directions:
1. Insert the Crisper Basket and close the hood. Select AIR CRISP, set the temperature to 390ºF, and set the time to 5 minutes. Select START/STOP to begin preheating.
2. Remove the crusts from the bread and flatten the slices with a rolling pin. Don't be gentle. Press hard so that bread will be very thin.
3. Top bread slices with cheese and chopped apple, dividing the ingredients evenly.
4. Roll up each slice tightly and secure each with one or two toothpicks.
5. Brush outside of rolls with melted butter.
6. Place in the Crisper Basket. Close the hood and AIR CRISP for 4 to 5 minutes, or until outside is crisp and nicely browned.
7. Serve hot.

Sweet Potato Fries With Honey-butter Sauce

Servings: 4 | Cooking Time: 20 Minutes

Ingredients:
- For the sweet potato fries
- 2 medium sweet potatoes, cut into ¼-inch-thick slices
- 3 teaspoons avocado oil
- 1 teaspoon salt
- ½ teaspoon paprika
- ½ teaspoon garlic powder
- ¼ teaspoon freshly ground black pepper
- For the honey butter
- 1 tablespoon honey
- 1 teaspoon powdered sugar
- 8 tablespoons (1 stick) salted butter, at room temperature

Directions:
1. Insert the Crisper Basket and close the hood. Select AIR CRISP, set the temperature to 400°F, and set the time to 20 minutes. Select START/STOP to begin preheating.
2. In a large bowl, drizzle the sweet potatoes with the avocado oil and toss to coat. In a small bowl, mix together the salt, paprika, garlic powder, and pepper. Sprinkle the seasoning over the sweet potatoes and toss gently to coat.
3. When the unit beeps to signify it has preheated, place the sweet potato fries in the Crisper Basket. Close the hood and cook for 10 minutes.
4. After 10 minutes, open the hood and shake the basket. Close the hood and cook for 5 minutes more. Open the hood again and shake the basket. If the fries are to your desired crispness, then remove them. If not, close the hood and cook up to 5 minutes more.
5. In a small bowl, whisk together the honey and powdered sugar until the sugar is dissolved. Add the butter and continue whisking. Serve alongside the fries.

Grilled Shishito Peppers

Servings: 4 | Cooking Time: 10 Minutes

Ingredients:
- 3 cups whole shishito peppers
- 2 tablespoons vegetable oil
- Flaky sea salt, for garnish

Directions:
1. Insert the Grill Grate and close the hood. Select GRILL, set the temperature to MAX, and set the time to 10 minutes. Select START/STOP to begin preheating.
2. While the unit is preheating, in a medium bowl, toss the peppers in the oil until evenly coated.
3. When the unit beeps to signify it has preheated, place the peppers on the Grill Grate. Gently press the peppers down to maximize grill marks. Close the hood and GRILL for 8 to 10 minutes, until they are blistered on all sides.
4. When cooking is complete, place the peppers in a serving dish and top with the flaky sea salt. Serve immediately.

Blistered Lemony Green Beans

Servings: 4 | Cooking Time: 10 Minutes

Ingredients:
- 1 pound haricots verts or green beans, trimmed
- 2 tablespoons vegetable oil
- Juice of 1 lemon
- Pinch red pepper flakes
- Flaky sea salt, to taste
- Freshly ground black pepper, to taste

Directions:
1. Insert the Grill Grate and close the hood. Select GRILL, set the temperature to MAX, and set the time to 10 minutes. Select START/STOP to begin preheating.
2. While the unit is preheating, in a medium bowl, toss the green beans in oil until evenly coated.
3. When the unit beeps to signify it has preheated, place the green beans on the Grill Grate. Close the hood and GRILL for 8 to 10 minutes, tossing frequently until blistered on all sides.
4. When cooking is complete, place the green beans on a large serving platter. Squeeze lemon juice over the green beans, top with red pepper flakes, and season with sea salt and black pepper.

Cheesy Steak Fries

Servings: 5 | Cooking Time: 20 Minutes

Ingredients:
- 1 bag frozen steak fries
- Cooking spray
- Salt and pepper, to taste
- ½ cup beef gravy
- 1 cup shredded Mozzarella cheese
- 2 scallions, green parts only, chopped

Directions:
1. Insert the Crisper Basket and close the hood. Select AIR CRISP, set the temperature to 400ºF, and set the time to 20 minutes. Select START/STOP to begin preheating.
2. Place the frozen steak fries in the basket. Close the hood and AIR CRISP for 10 minutes. Shake the basket and spritz the fries with cooking spray. Sprinkle with salt and pepper. AIR CRISP for an additional 8 minutes.
3. Pour the beef gravy into a medium, microwave-safe bowl. Microwave for 30 seconds, or until the gravy is warm.
4. Sprinkle the fries with the cheese. Close the hood and AIR CRISP for an additional 2 minutes, until the cheese is melted.
5. Transfer the fries to a serving dish. Drizzle the fries with gravy and sprinkle the scallions on top for a green garnish. Serve.

Balsamic Broccoli

Servings: 4 | Cooking Time: 10 Minutes

Ingredients:
- 4 tablespoons soy sauce
- 4 tablespoons balsamic vinegar
- 2 tablespoons canola oil
- 2 teaspoons maple syrup
- 2 heads broccoli, trimmed into florets
- Red pepper flakes, for garnish
- Sesame seeds, for garnish

Directions:
1. Insert the Grill Grate and close the hood. Select GRILL, set the temperature to MAX, and set the time to 10 minutes. Select START/STOP to begin preheating.
2. While the unit is preheating, in a large bowl, whisk together the soy sauce, balsamic vinegar, oil, and maple syrup. Add the broccoli and toss to coat evenly.
3. When the unit beeps to signify it has preheated, place the broccoli on the Grill Grate. Close the hood and GRILL for 8 to 10 minutes, until charred on all sides.
4. When cooking is complete, place the broccoli on a large serving platter. Garnish with red pepper flakes and sesame seeds. Serve immediately.

Maple Butter Corn Bread

Servings: 4 | Cooking Time: 40 Minutes

Ingredients:

- For the corn bread
- 1 cup all-purpose flour
- 1 cup yellow cornmeal
- 2 teaspoons baking powder
- 1 teaspoon salt
- 1¼ cups milk
- ⅓ cup canola oil
- 1 large egg
- 1 (14.75-ounce) can cream-style sweet corn
- Cooking spray
- For the maple butter
- 1 tablespoon light brown sugar, packed
- 1 tablespoon milk
- 8 tablespoons (1 stick) unsalted butter, at room temperature
- 1 tablespoon maple syrup

Directions:

1. Insert the Cooking Pot and close the hood. Select BAKE, set the temperature to 350°F, and set the time to 40 minutes. Select START/STOP to begin preheating.
2. While the unit is preheating, in a large bowl, combine the flour, cornmeal, baking powder, salt, milk, oil, egg, and sweet corn. Mix until just combined. Grease a 9-by-5-inch loaf pan with cooking spray and pour in the corn bread batter.
3. When the unit beeps to signify it has preheated, place the pan in the Cooking Pot. Close the hood and cook for 40 minutes. If using a metal loaf pan, check the corn bread after 30 minutes, as metal pans may cook faster than glass. Bake until golden brown and the mix is completely baked through.
4. When cooking is complete, the corn bread should be golden brown and a toothpick inserted into the center of the corn bread comes out clean. Remove the pan from the grill and set aside to cool.
5. In a small bowl, whisk together the brown sugar and milk until the sugar is dissolved. Add the butter and continue whisking. Add the maple syrup and continue whisking until fully combined.
6. Cut the corn bread into slices, top with the butter, and serve.

Bruschetta With Tomato And Basil

Servings: 6 | Cooking Time: 6 Minutes

Ingredients:

- 4 tomatoes, diced
- ⅓ cup shredded fresh basil
- ¼ cup shredded Parmesan cheese
- 1 tablespoon balsamic vinegar
- 1 tablespoon minced garlic
- 1 teaspoon olive oil
- 1 teaspoon salt
- 1 teaspoon freshly ground black pepper
- 1 loaf French bread, cut into 1-inch-thick slices
- Cooking spray

Directions:

1. Insert the Crisper Basket and close the hood. Select BAKE, set the temperature to 250ºF, and set the time to 3 minutes. Select START/STOP to begin preheating.
2. Mix together the tomatoes and basil in a medium bowl. Add the cheese, vinegar, garlic, olive oil, salt, and pepper and stir until well incorporated. Set aside.
3. Spritz the Crisper Basket with cooking spray. Working in batches, lay the bread slices in the basket in a single layer. Spray the slices with cooking spray.
4. Close the hood and BAKE for 3 minutes until golden brown.
5. Remove from the basket to a plate. Repeat with the remaining bread slices.
6. Top each slice with a generous spoonful of the tomato mixture and serve.

Cayenne Sesame Nut Mix

Servings:4 | Cooking Time: 2 Minutes

Ingredients:
- 1 tablespoon buttery spread, melted
- 2 teaspoons honey
- ¼ teaspoon cayenne pepper
- 2 teaspoons sesame seeds
- ¼ teaspoon kosher salt
- ¼ teaspoon freshly ground black pepper
- 1 cup cashews
- 1 cup almonds
- 1 cup mini pretzels
- 1 cup rice squares cereal
- Cooking spray

Directions:
1. Select BAKE, set the temperature to 360ºF, and set the time to 2 minutes. Select START/STOP to begin preheating.
2. In a large bowl, combine the buttery spread, honey, cayenne pepper, sesame seeds, kosher salt, and black pepper, then add the cashews, almonds, pretzels, and rice squares, tossing to coat.
3. Spray a baking pan with cooking spray, then pour the mixture into the pan. Place the pan directly in the pot. Close the hood and BAKE for 2 minutes.
4. Remove the sesame mix from the grill and allow to cool in the pan on a wire rack for 5 minutes before serving.

Cheese And Ham Stuffed Baby Bella

Servings: 8 | Cooking Time: 12 Minutes

Ingredients:
- 4 ounces Mozzarella cheese, cut into pieces
- ½ cup diced ham
- 2 green onions, chopped
- 2 tablespoons bread crumbs
- ½ teaspoon garlic powder
- ¼ teaspoon ground oregano
- ¼ teaspoon ground black pepper
- 1 to 2 teaspoons olive oil
- 16 fresh Baby Bella mushrooms, stemmed removed

Directions:
1. Process the cheese, ham, green onions, bread crumbs, garlic powder, oregano, and pepper in a food processor until finely chopped.
2. With the food processor running, slowly drizzle in 1 to 2 teaspoons olive oil until a thick paste has formed. Transfer the mixture to a bowl.
3. Evenly divide the mixture into the mushroom caps and lightly press down the mixture.
4. Insert the Crisper Basket and close the hood. Select ROAST, set the temperature to 390ºF, and set the time to 12 minutes. Select START/STOP to begin preheating.
5. Lay the mushrooms in the Crisper Basket in a single layer. You'll need to work in batches to avoid overcrowding.
6. Close the hood and ROAST for 12 minutes until the mushrooms are lightly browned and tender.
7. Remove from the basket to a plate and repeat with the remaining mushrooms.
8. Let the mushrooms cool for 5 minutes and serve warm.

Desserts

Mini Brownie Cakes

Servings:4 | Cooking Time: 15 Minutes

Ingredients:
- 8 tablespoons (1 stick) unsalted butter
- 2 large eggs
- ¼ cup unsweetened cocoa powder
- ½ cup granulated sugar
- ½ teaspoon vanilla extract
- ⅛ teaspoon salt
- ½ cup all-purpose flour

Directions:
1. Cut the butter into quarters and divide them between 2 (6-ounce) ramekins. Insert the Cooking Pot, place the ramekins in the pot, and close the hood. Select GRILL, set the temperature to LO, and set the time to 15 minutes. Select START/STOP to begin preheating. After 3 minutes of preheating (set a separate timer), use grill mitts to remove the ramekins and set aside. Close the hood to continue preheating.
2. While the unit is preheating, in a large bowl, whisk the eggs together, then add the cocoa powder, sugar, vanilla, and salt. Sift or gradually shake the flour into the bowl as you continue mixing. Then stir in the melted butter to form a smooth batter. Divide the batter evenly among 4 (6-ounce) ramekins, filling them no more than three-quarters full.
3. When the unit beeps to signify it has preheated, place the ramekins in the Cooking Pot. Close the hood and cook for 15 minutes.
4. When cooking is complete, open the hood and remove the ramekins. The brownies are done when a toothpick inserted in the center comes out clean. (Cooking them for 15 minutes usually gives the brownies a crispy crust with a fudgy center. Add another 3 to 5 minutes if you wish to cook the center all the way through.)

Fresh Blueberry Cobbler

Servings: 6 | Cooking Time: 30 Minutes

Ingredients:
- 4 cups fresh blueberries
- 1 teaspoon grated lemon zest
- 1 cup sugar, plus 2 tablespoons
- 1 cup all-purpose flour, plus 2 tablespoons
- Juice of 1 lemon
- 2 teaspoons baking powder
- ¼ teaspoon salt
- 6 tablespoons unsalted butter
- ¾ cup whole milk
- ⅛ teaspoon ground cinnamon

Directions:
1. In a medium bowl, combine the blueberries, lemon zest, 2 tablespoons of sugar, 2 tablespoons of flour, and lemon juice.
2. In a medium bowl, combine the remaining 1 cup of flour and 1 cup of sugar, baking powder, and salt. Cut the butter into the flour mixture until it forms an even crumb texture. Stir in the milk until a dough forms.
3. Select BAKE, set the temperature to 350°F, and set the time to 30 minutes. Select START/STOP to begin preheating.
4. Meanwhile, pour the blueberry mixture into the baking pan, spreading it evenly across the pan. Gently pour the batter over the blueberry mixture, then sprinkle the cinnamon over the top.
5. When the unit beeps to signify it has preheated, place the pan directly in the pot. Close the hood and BAKE for 30 minutes, until lightly golden.
6. When cooking is complete, serve warm.

Simple Corn Biscuits

Servings: 6 | Cooking Time: 15 Minutes

Ingredients:
- 1½ cups all-purpose flour, plus additional for dusting
- ½ cup yellow cornmeal
- 2½ teaspoons baking powder
- ½ teaspoon sea salt
- ⅓ cup vegetable shortening
- ⅔ cup buttermilk
- Nonstick cooking spray

Directions:
1. In a large bowl, combine the flour, cornmeal, baking powder, and salt.
2. Add the shortening, and cut it into the flour mixture, until well combined and the dough resembles a coarse meal. Add the buttermilk and stir together just until moistened.
3. Insert the Crisper Basket and close the hood. Select AIR CRISP, set the temperature to 350ºF, and set the time to 15 minutes. Select START/STOP to begin preheating.
4. While the unit is preheating, dust a clean work surface with flour. Knead the mixture on the floured surface until a cohesive dough forms. Roll out the dough to an even thickness, then cut into biscuits with a 2-inch biscuit cutter.
5. When the unit beeps to signify it has preheated, coat the basket with cooking spray. Place 6 to 8 biscuits in the basket, well spaced, and spray each with cooking spray. Close the hood and AIR CRISP for 12 to 15 minutes, until golden brown.
6. Gently remove the biscuits from the basket, and place them on a wire rack to cool. Repeat with the remaining dough.

Vanilla Scones

Servings:18 | Cooking Time: 15 Minutes

Ingredients:
- For the scones
- 2 cups almond flour
- ¼ cup granulated sugar
- ¼ teaspoon salt
- 1 tablespoon baking powder
- 2 large eggs
- 1 teaspoon vanilla extract
- 4 tablespoons (½ stick) unsalted butter, melted
- 2 tablespoons heavy (whipping) cream
- For the icing
- 1 cup powdered sugar
- 2 tablespoons heavy (whipping) cream
- 1 tablespoon vanilla extract

Directions:
1. In a large bowl, combine the almond flour, granulated sugar, salt, and baking powder. In another large bowl, whisk the eggs, then whisk in the vanilla, butter, and heavy cream. Add the dry ingredients to the wet and mix just until a dough forms.
2. Insert the Cooking Pot and close the hood. Select BAKE, set the temperature to 325°F, and set the time to 15 minutes. Select START/STOP to begin preheating.
3. While the unit is preheating, divide the dough into 3 equal pieces. Shape each piece into a disc about 1 inch thick and 5 inches in diameter. Cut each into 6 wedges, like slicing a pizza.
4. When the unit beeps to signify it has preheated, place the scones in the Cooking Pot, spacing them apart so they don't bake together. Close the hood and cook for 15 minutes.
5. While the scones are baking, in a small bowl, combine the powdered sugar, heavy cream, and vanilla. Stir until smooth.
6. After 15 minutes, open the hood and remove the scones. They are done baking when they have turned a light golden brown. Place on a wire rack to cool to room temperature. Drizzle the icing over the scones, or pour a tablespoonful on the top of each scone for an even glaze.

Orange And Anise Cake

Servings: 6 | Cooking Time: 20 Minutes

Ingredients:
- 1 stick butter, at room temperature
- 5 tablespoons liquid monk fruit
- 2 eggs plus 1 egg yolk, beaten
- ⅓ cup hazelnuts, roughly chopped
- 3 tablespoons sugar-free orange marmalade
- 6 ounces unbleached almond flour
- 1 teaspoon baking soda
- ½ teaspoon baking powder
- ½ teaspoon ground cinnamon
- ½ teaspoon ground allspice
- ½ ground anise seed
- Cooking spray

Directions:
1. Select BAKE, set the temperature to 310°F, and set the time to 20 minutes. Select START/STOP to begin preheating.
2. Lightly spritz a baking pan with cooking spray.
3. In a mixing bowl, whisk the butter and liquid monk fruit until the mixture is pale and smooth. Mix in the beaten eggs, hazelnuts, and marmalade and whisk again until well incorporated.
4. Add the almond flour, baking soda, baking powder, cinnamon, allspice, anise seed and stir to mix well.
5. Scrape the batter into the prepared baking pan. Place the pan directly in the pot. Close the hood and BAKE for 20 minutes, or until the top of the cake springs back when gently pressed with your fingers.
6. Transfer to a wire rack and let the cake cool to room temperature. Serve immediately.

Grilled Apple Fries With Caramel Cream Cheese Dip

Servings: 4 | Cooking Time: 5 Minutes

Ingredients:
- 4 apples, such as Honeycrisp, Gala, Pink Lady, or Granny Smith, peeled, cored, and sliced
- ¼ cup heavy (whipping) cream
- 1 tablespoon granulated sugar
- ¼ teaspoon cinnamon
- ¼ cup all-purpose flour
- 4 ounces cream cheese, at room temperature
- 1 tablespoon caramel sauce
- 1 tablespoon light brown sugar, packed

Directions:
1. Insert the Grill Grate and close the hood. Select GRILL, set the temperature to MAX, and set the time to 5 minutes. Select START/STOP to begin preheating.
2. In a large bowl, toss the apple slices with the heavy cream, granulated sugar, and cinnamon to coat. Slowly shake in the flour and continue mixing to coat.
3. In a small bowl, mix together the cream cheese, caramel sauce, and brown sugar until smooth. Set aside.
4. When the unit beeps to signify it has preheated, place the apples on the Grill Grate in a single layer. Close the hood and grill for 2 minutes, 30 seconds.
5. After 2 minutes, 30 seconds, open the hood and flip and toss the apples around. Close the hood and cook for 2 minutes, 30 seconds more.
6. When cooking is complete, open the hood and remove the apple chips from the grill. Serve with the sauce.

Rich Chocolate Cookie

Servings: 4 | Cooking Time: 9 Minutes

Ingredients:
- Nonstick baking spray with flour
- 3 tablespoons softened butter
- ⅓ cup plus 1 tablespoon brown sugar
- 1 egg yolk
- ½ cup flour
- 2 tablespoons ground white chocolate
- ¼ teaspoon baking soda
- ½ teaspoon vanilla
- ¾ cup chocolate chips

Directions:
1. Select BAKE, set the temperature to 350°F, and set the time to 9 minutes. Select START/STOP to begin preheating.
2. In a medium bowl, beat the butter and brown sugar together until fluffy. Stir in the egg yolk.
3. Add the flour, white chocolate, baking soda, and vanilla, and mix well. Stir in the chocolate chips.
4. Line a baking pan with parchment paper. Spray the parchment paper with nonstick baking spray with flour.
5. Spread the batter into the prepared pan, leaving a ½-inch border on all sides.
6. Place the pan directly in the pot. Close the hood and BAKE for 9 minutes or until the cookie is light brown and just barely set.
7. Remove the pan from the grill and let cool for 10 minutes. Remove the cookie from the pan, remove the parchment paper, and let cool on a wire rack.
8. Serve immediately.

Chocolate And Coconut Cake

Servings: 6 | Cooking Time: 15 Minutes

Ingredients:
- ½ cup unsweetened chocolate, chopped
- ½ stick butter, at room temperature
- 1 tablespoon liquid stevia
- 1½ cups coconut flour
- 2 eggs, whisked
- ½ teaspoon vanilla extract
- A pinch of fine sea salt
- Cooking spray

Directions:
1. Place the chocolate, butter, and stevia in a microwave-safe bowl. Microwave for about 30 seconds until melted.
2. Let the chocolate mixture cool for 5 to 10 minutes.
3. Add the remaining ingredients to the bowl of chocolate mixture and whisk to incorporate.
4. Select BAKE, set the temperature to 330°F, and set the time to 15 minutes. Select START/STOP to begin preheating.
5. Lightly spray a baking pan with cooking spray.
6. Scrape the chocolate mixture into the prepared baking pan.
7. Place the pan directly in the pot. Close the hood and BAKE for 15 minutes, or until the top springs back lightly when gently pressed with your fingers.
8. Let the cake cool for 5 minutes and serve.

Pineapple And Chocolate Cake

Servings: 4 | Cooking Time: 35 To 40 Minutes

Ingredients:

- 2 cups flour
- 4 ounces butter, melted
- ¼ cup sugar
- ½ pound pineapple, chopped
- ½ cup pineapple juice
- 1 ounce dark chocolate, grated
- 1 large egg
- 2 tablespoons skimmed milk

Directions:

1. Select BAKE, set the temperature to 370ºF, and set the time to 40 minutes. Select START/STOP to begin preheating.
2. Grease a cake tin with a little oil or butter.
3. In a bowl, combine the butter and flour to create a crumbly consistency.
4. Add the sugar, chopped pineapple, juice, and grated dark chocolate and mix well.
5. In a separate bowl, combine the egg and milk. Add this mixture to the flour mixture and stir well until a soft dough forms.
6. Pour the mixture into the cake tin and transfer to the grill.
7. Close the hood and BAKE for 35 to 40 minutes.
8. Serve immediately.

Chocolate Coconut Brownies

Servings: 8 | Cooking Time: 15 Minutes

Ingredients:

- ½ cup coconut oil
- 2 ounces dark chocolate
- 1 cup sugar
- 2½ tablespoons water
- 4 whisked eggs
- ¼ teaspoon ground cinnamon
- ½ teaspoons ground anise star
- ¼ teaspoon coconut extract
- ½ teaspoons vanilla extract
- 1 tablespoon honey
- ½ cup flour
- ½ cup desiccated coconut
- Sugar, for dusting

Directions:

1. Select BAKE, set the temperature to 355ºF, and set the time to 15 minutes. Select START/STOP to begin preheating.
2. Melt the coconut oil and dark chocolate in the microwave.
3. Combine with the sugar, water, eggs, cinnamon, anise, coconut extract, vanilla, and honey in a large bowl.
4. Stir in the flour and desiccated coconut. Incorporate everything well.
5. Lightly grease a baking pan with butter. Transfer the mixture to the pan.
6. Place the pan directly in the pot. Close the hood and BAKE for 15 minutes.
7. Remove from the grill and allow to cool slightly.
8. Take care when taking it out of the baking pan. Slice it into squares.
9. Dust with sugar before serving.

Fudge Pie

Servings: 8 | Cooking Time: 25 To 30 Minutes

Ingredients:

- 1½ cups sugar
- ½ cup self-rising flour
- ⅓ cup unsweetened cocoa powder
- 3 large eggs, beaten
- 12 tablespoons butter, melted
- 1½ teaspoons vanilla extract
- 1 unbaked pie crust
- ¼ cup confectioners' sugar (optional)

Directions:

1. Select BAKE, set the temperature to 350ºF, and set the time to 30 minutes. Select START/STOP to begin preheating.
2. Thoroughly combine the sugar, flour, and cocoa powder in a medium bowl. Add the beaten eggs and butter and whisk to combine. Stir in the vanilla.
3. Pour the prepared filling into the pie crust and transfer to the pot.
4. Close the hood and BAKE for 25 to 30 minutes until just set.
5. Allow the pie to cool for 5 minutes. Sprinkle with the confectioners' sugar, if desired. Serve warm.

Biscuit Raisin Bread

Servings: 6 To 8 | Cooking Time: 20 Minutes

Ingredients:
- 1 (12-ounce) package refrigerated buttermilk biscuits (10 biscuits)
- 8 ounces cream cheese, cut into 40 cubes
- ¼ cup light brown sugar, packed
- 4 tablespoons (½ stick) unsalted butter, melted
- ½ cup raisins

Directions:
1. Insert the Cooking Pot and close the hood. Select GRILL, set the temperature to LO, and set the time to 20 minutes. Select START/STOP to begin preheating.
2. While the unit is preheating, separate the biscuits and cut each into quarters. Flatten each quarter biscuit with your palm and place 1 cream cheese cube on the center. Wrap the dough around the cream cheese and press to seal, forming a ball. Place the biscuit balls in a 9-by-5-inch bread loaf pan. They will be layered over each other.
3. In a small bowl, combine the brown sugar and melted butter. Pour this over the biscuit balls evenly.
4. When the unit beeps to signify it has preheated, place the loaf pan in the Cooking Pot. Close the hood and grill for 10 minutes.
5. After 10 minutes, open the hood and evenly scatter the raisins on the top layer. Close the hood and cook for 10 minutes more.
6. When cooking is complete, remove the loaf pan from the pot. Remove the bread from the pan, slice, and serve.

Blackberry Chocolate Cake

Servings: 8 | Cooking Time: 22 Minutes

Ingredients:
- ½ cup butter, at room temperature
- 2 ounces Swerve
- 4 eggs
- 1 cup almond flour
- 1 teaspoon baking soda
- ⅓ teaspoon baking powder
- ½ cup cocoa powder
- 1 teaspoon orange zest
- ⅓ cup fresh blackberries

Directions:
1. Select BAKE, set the temperature to 335ºF, and set the time to 22 minutes. Select START/STOP to begin preheating.
2. With an electric mixer or hand mixer, beat the butter and Swerve until creamy.
3. One at a time, mix in the eggs and beat again until fluffy.
4. Add the almond flour, baking soda, baking powder, cocoa powder, orange zest and mix well. Add the butter mixture to the almond flour mixture and stir until well blended. Fold in the blackberries.
5. Scrape the batter to a baking pan. Place the pan directly in the pot. Close the hood and BAKE for 22 minutes. Check the cake for doneness: If a toothpick inserted into the center of the cake comes out clean, it's done.
6. Allow the cake cool on a wire rack to room temperature. Serve immediately.

Chocolate Pecan Pie

Servings: 8 | Cooking Time: 25 Minutes

Ingredients:
- 1 unbaked pie crust
- Filling:
- 2 large eggs
- ⅓ cup butter, melted
- 1 cup sugar
- ½ cup all-purpose flour
- 1 cup milk chocolate chips
- 1½ cups coarsely chopped pecans
- 2 tablespoons bourbon

Directions:
1. Select BAKE, set the temperature to 350°F, and set the time to 25 minutes. Select START/STOP to begin preheating.
2. Whisk the eggs and melted butter in a large bowl until creamy.
3. Add the sugar and flour and stir to incorporate. Mix in the milk chocolate chips, pecans, and bourbon and stir until well combined.
4. Use a fork to prick holes in the bottom and sides of the pie crust. Pour the prepared filling into the pie crust. Place the pie crust in the pot.
5. Close the hood and BAKE for 25 minutes until a toothpick inserted in the center comes out clean.
6. Allow the pie cool for 10 minutes in the basket before serving.

Apple Pie Crumble

Servings: 4 | Cooking Time: 20 Minutes

Ingredients:
- 3 small apples, such as Honeycrisp, Gala, Pink Lady, or Granny Smith, peeled, cored, and cut into ⅛-inch-thick slices
- ¼ cup granulated sugar
- ½ teaspoon cinnamon
- ½ cup quick-cooking oatmeal
- 4 tablespoons (½ stick) unsalted butter, at room temperature
- ½ cup all-purpose flour
- ½ cup light brown sugar, packed

Directions:
1. Insert the Cooking Pot and close the hood. Select GRILL, set the temperature to LO, and set the time to 20 minutes. Select START/STOP to begin preheating.
2. While the unit is preheating, put the apples in a large bowl and coat with the granulated sugar and cinnamon. In a medium bowl, combine the oatmeal, butter, flour, and brown sugar, stirring to make clumps for the top layer.
3. Place the apples in a 6-inch springform pan in an even layer. Spread the oatmeal topping over the apples.
4. When the unit beeps to signify it has preheated, place the pan in the Cooking Pot. Close the hood and cook for 20 minutes.
5. After 20 minutes, open the hood and remove the pan from the unit. The apples should be soft and the topping golden brown. Serve.

Pumpkin Pudding

Servings: 4 | Cooking Time: 15 Minutes

Ingredients:
- 3 cups pumpkin purée
- 3 tablespoons honey
- 1 tablespoon ginger
- 1 tablespoon cinnamon
- 1 teaspoon clove
- 1 teaspoon nutmeg
- 1 cup full-fat cream
- 2 eggs
- 1 cup sugar

Directions:
1. Select BAKE, set the temperature to 390°F, and set the time to 15 minutes. Select START/STOP to begin preheating.
2. In a bowl, stir all the ingredients together to combine.
3. Scrape the mixture into a greased baking pan. Place the pan directly in the pot. Close the hood and BAKE for 15 minutes.
4. Serve warm.

Graham Cracker Cheesecake

Servings: 8 | Cooking Time: 20 Minutes

Ingredients:
- 1 cup graham cracker crumbs
- 3 tablespoons softened butter
- 1½ packages cream cheese, softened
- ⅓ cup sugar
- 2 eggs
- 1 tablespoon flour
- 1 teaspoon vanilla
- ¼ cup chocolate syrup

Directions:
1. For the crust, combine the graham cracker crumbs and butter in a small bowl and mix well. Press into the bottom of a baking pan and put in the freezer to set.
2. For the filling, combine the cream cheese and sugar in a medium bowl and mix well. Beat in the eggs, one at a time. Add the flour and vanilla.
3. Select BAKE, set the temperature to 450°F, and set the time to 20 minutes. Select START/STOP to begin preheating.
4. Remove ⅔ cup of the filling to a small bowl and stir in the chocolate syrup until combined.
5. Pour the vanilla filling into the pan with the crust. Drop the chocolate filling over the vanilla filling by the spoonful. With a clean butter knife, stir the fillings in a zigzag pattern to marbleize them.
6. Place the pan directly in the pot. Close the hood and BAKE for 20 minutes or until the cheesecake is just set.
7. Cool on a wire rack for 1 hour, then chill in the refrigerator until the cheesecake is firm.
8. Serve immediately.

Candied Pecans

Servings: 4 | Cooking Time: 20 Minutes

Ingredients:
- 1 large egg white
- 1 teaspoon vanilla extract
- 1 tablespoon water
- ¼ cup granulated sugar
- ¼ cup light brown sugar, packed
- 1 teaspoon ground cinnamon
- 1 teaspoon salt
- 1 pound pecan halves

Directions:
1. Insert the Cooking Pot and close the hood. Select GRILL, set the temperature to MED, and set the time to 20 minutes. Select START/STOP to begin preheating.
2. While the unit is preheating, in a large bowl, whisk together the egg white, vanilla, and water until it becomes frothy.
3. In a small bowl, combine the granulated sugar, brown sugar, cinnamon, and salt. Add the pecans to the egg mixture, coating them well. Then add the sugar mixture and stir to coat the pecans evenly.
4. When the unit beeps to signify it has preheated, evenly spread the pecans in the Cooking Pot. Close the hood and grill for 5 minutes.
5. After 5 minutes, open the hood and stir the pecans. Close the hood and cook for 5 minutes. Repeat until the pecans have cooked for 20 minutes total.
6. When cooking is complete, remove the pecans from the Cooking Pot and spread them on a baking sheet to cool to room temperature. Store in a resealable bag or airtight container.

Everyday Cheesecake

Servings: 4 | Cooking Time: 35 Minutes

Ingredients:
- 1 large egg
- 8 ounces cream cheese, at room temperature
- ¼ cup heavy (whipping) cream
- ¼ cup sour cream
- ¼ cup powdered sugar
- 1 teaspoon vanilla extract
- 5 ounces cookies, such as chocolate, vanilla, cinnamon, or your favorite
- 4 tablespoons (½ stick) unsalted butter, melted

Directions:
1. In a large bowl, whisk the egg. Then add the cream cheese, heavy cream, and sour cream and whisk until smooth. Slowly add the powdered sugar and vanilla, whisking until fully mixed.
2. Insert the Cooking Pot and close the hood. Select BAKE, set the temperature to 350°F, and set the time to 35 minutes. Select START/STOP to begin preheating.
3. While the unit is preheating, crush the cookies into fine crumbs. Place them in a 6-inch springform pan and drizzle evenly with the melted butter. Using your fingers, press down on the crumbs to form a crust on the bottom of the pan. Pour the cream cheese mixture on top of the crust. Cover the pan with aluminum foil, making sure the foil fully covers the sides of the pan and tucks under the bottom so it does not lift up and block the Splatter Shield as the air flows while baking.
4. When the unit beeps to signify it has preheated, place the springform pan in the Cooking Pot. Close the hood and cook for 25 minutes.
5. After 25 minutes, open the hood and remove the foil. Close the hood and cook for 10 minutes more.
6. When cooking is complete, remove the pan from the Cooking Pot and let the cheesecake cool for 1 hour, then place the cheesecake in the refrigerator for at least 3 hours. Slice and serve.

Rum Grilled Pineapple Sundaes

Servings: 6 | Cooking Time: 8 Minutes

Ingredients:
- ½ cup dark rum
- ½ cup packed brown sugar
- 1 teaspoon ground cinnamon, plus more for garnish
- 1 pineapple, cored and sliced
- Vanilla ice cream, for serving

Directions:
1. In a large shallow bowl or storage container, combine the rum, sugar, and cinnamon. Add the pineapple slices and arrange them in a single layer. Coat with the mixture, then let soak for at least 5 minutes per side.
2. Insert the Grill Grate and close the hood. Select GRILL, set the temperature to MAX, and set the time to 8 minutes. Select START/STOP to begin preheating.
3. While the unit is preheating, strain the extra rum sauce from the pineapple.
4. When the unit beeps to signify it has preheated, place the fruit on the Grill Grate in a single layer (you may need to do this in multiple batches). Gently press the fruit down to maximize grill marks. Close the hood and GRILL for about 6 to 8 minutes without flipping. If working in batches, remove the pineapple, and repeat this step for the remaining pineapple slices.
5. When cooking is complete, remove, and top each pineapple ring with a scoop of ice cream. Sprinkle with cinnamon and serve immediately.

Coffee Chocolate Cake

Servings: 8 | Cooking Time: 30 Minutes

Ingredients:
- Dry Ingredients:
- 1½ cups almond flour
- ½ cup coconut meal
- ⅔ cup Swerve
- 1 teaspoon baking powder
- ¼ teaspoon salt

- Wet Ingredients:
- 1 egg
- 1 stick butter, melted
- ½ cup hot strongly brewed coffee
- Topping:
- ½ cup confectioner's Swerve
- ¼ cup coconut flour
- 3 tablespoons coconut oil
- 1 teaspoon ground cinnamon
- ½ teaspoon ground cardamom

Directions:
1. Select BAKE, set the temperature to 330°F, and set the time to 30 minutes. Select START/STOP to begin preheating.
2. In a medium bowl, combine the almond flour, coconut meal, Swerve, baking powder, and salt.
3. In a large bowl, whisk the egg, melted butter, and coffee until smooth.
4. Add the dry mixture to the wet and stir until well incorporated. Transfer the batter to a greased baking pan.
5. Stir together all the ingredients for the topping in a small bowl. Spread the topping over the batter and smooth the top with a spatula.
6. Place the pan directly in the pot. Close the hood and BAKE for 30 minutes, or until the cake springs back when gently pressed with your fingers.
7. Rest for 10 minutes before serving.

Black Forest Pies

Servings: 6 | Cooking Time: 15 Minutes

Ingredients:
- 3 tablespoons milk or dark chocolate chips
- 2 tablespoons thick, hot fudge sauce
- 2 tablespoons chopped dried cherries
- 1 sheet frozen puff pastry, thawed
- 1 egg white, beaten
- 2 tablespoons sugar
- ½ teaspoon cinnamon

Directions:
1. Insert the Crisper Basket and close the hood. Select BAKE, set the temperature to 350°F, and set the time to 15 minutes. Select START/STOP to begin preheating.
2. In a small bowl, combine the chocolate chips, fudge sauce, and dried cherries.
3. Roll out the puff pastry on a floured surface. Cut into 6 squares with a sharp knife.
4. Divide the chocolate chip mixture into the center of each puff pastry square. Fold the squares in half to make triangles. Firmly press the edges with the tines of a fork to seal.
5. Brush the triangles on all sides sparingly with the beaten egg white. Sprinkle the tops with sugar and cinnamon.
6. Put in the Crisper Basket. Close the hood and BAKE for 15 minutes or until the triangles are golden brown. The filling will be hot, so cool for at least 20 minutes before serving.

Pecan Pie

Servings: 4 | Cooking Time: 20 Minutes

Ingredients:
- 6 ounces cream cheese, at room temperature
- 4 tablespoons (½ stick) unsalted butter
- 2 large eggs
- 1 teaspoon vanilla extract
- 1 cup light brown sugar, packed
- 1 cup all-purpose flour
- ½ cup pecan halves

Directions:
1. Place the cream cheese and butter in a 7-inch silicone cake pan. Insert the Cooking Pot, place the cake pan in the pot, and close the hood. Select BAKE, set the temperature to 350°F, and set the time to 20 minutes. (If using a metal or glass cake pan, you may need to add 5 to 10 minutes to the baking time.) Select START/STOP to begin preheating. After 5 minutes of preheating (set a separate timer), open the hood and remove the cake pan. (The cream cheese and butter will be melted but not combined.) Close the hood to continue preheating.
2. While the unit is preheating, in a medium bowl, whisk together the eggs, vanilla, brown sugar, and 1½ tablespoons of the melted butter from the cake pan.
3. Transfer the remaining butter and cream cheese from the cake pan to a large bowl and mix to combine. (It may look a little like cottage cheese.) Slowly sift the flour into the bowl. Begin kneading and mixing the dough together with your hands. It may be sticky at first, but continue mixing until it forms into a smooth dough. Place the dough in the cake pan and press it into the bottom and up the sides of the pan to form a piecrust.
4. Pour the filling into the piecrust and top with the pecans.
5. When the unit beeps to signify it has preheated, place the cake pan in the Cooking Pot. Close the hood and bake for 20 minutes.
6. When cooking is complete, the crust edges will be golden brown. Remove the cake pan and let cool to room temperature before slicing and serving.

Marshmallow Banana Boat

Servings: 4 | Cooking Time: 6 Minutes

Ingredients:
- 4 ripe bananas
- 1 cup mini marshmallows
- ½ cup chocolate chips
- ½ cup peanut butter chips

Directions:
1. Insert the Grill Grate and close the hood. Select GRILL, set the temperature to MEDIUM, and set the time to 6 minutes. Select START/STOP to begin preheating.
2. While the unit is preheating, slice each banana lengthwise while still in its peel, making sure not to cut all the way through. Using both hands, pull the banana peel open like you would a book, revealing the banana inside. Divide the marshmallows, chocolate chips, and peanut butter chips among the bananas, stuffing them inside the skin.
3. When the unit beeps to signify it has preheated, place the stuffed banana on the Grill Grate. Close the hood and GRILL for 4 to 6 minutes, until the chocolate is melted and the marshmallows are toasted.

Curry Peaches, Pears, And Plums

Servings: 6 To 8 | Cooking Time: 5 Minutes

Ingredients:
- 2 peaches
- 2 firm pears
- 2 plums
- 2 tablespoons melted butter
- 1 tablespoon honey
- 2 to 3 teaspoons curry powder

Directions:
1. Insert the Crisper Basket and close the hood. Select BAKE, set the temperature to 325ºF, and set the time to 8 minutes. Select START/STOP to begin preheating.
2. Cut the peaches in half, remove the pits, and cut each half in half again. Cut the pears in half, core them, and remove the stem. Cut each half in half again. Do the same with the plums.
3. Spread a large sheet of heavy-duty foil on the work surface. Arrange the fruit on the foil and drizzle with the butter and honey. Sprinkle with the curry powder.
4. Wrap the fruit in the foil, making sure to leave some air space in the packet.
5. Put the foil package in the basket. Close the hood and BAKE for 5 to 8 minutes, shaking the basket once during the cooking time, until the fruit is soft.
6. Serve immediately.

Ultimate Skillet Brownies

Servings: 6 | Cooking Time: 40 Minutes

Ingredients:
- ½ cup all-purpose flour
- ¼ cup unsweetened cocoa powder
- ¾ teaspoon sea salt
- 2 large eggs
- 1 tablespoon water
- ½ cup granulated sugar
- ½ cup dark brown sugar
- 1 tablespoon vanilla extract
- 8 ounces semisweet chocolate chips, melted
- ¾ cup unsalted butter, melted
- Nonstick cooking spray

Directions:
1. In a medium bowl, whisk together the flour, cocoa powder, and salt.
2. In a large bowl, whisk together the eggs, water, sugar, brown sugar, and vanilla until smooth.
3. In a microwave-safe bowl, melt the chocolate in the microwave. In a separate microwave-safe bowl, melt the butter.
4. In a separate medium bowl, stir together the chocolate and butter until evenly combined. Whisk into the egg mixture. Then slowly add the dry ingredients, stirring just until incorporated.
5. Remove the Grill Grate from the unit. Select BAKE, set the temperature to 350ºF, and set the time to 40 minutes. Select START/STOP to begin preheating.
6. Meanwhile, lightly grease the baking pan with cooking spray. Pour the batter into the pan, spreading evenly.
7. When the unit beeps to signify it has preheated, place the pan directly in the pot. Close the hood and BAKE for 40 minutes.
8. After 40 minutes, check that baking is complete. A wooden toothpick inserted into the center of the brownies should come out clean.

Churros With Chocolate-yogurt Sauce

Servings: 8 | Cooking Time: 30 Minutes

Ingredients:

- 1 cup water
- 1 stick unsalted butter, cut into 8 pieces
- ½ cup sugar, plus 1 tablespoon
- 1 cup all-purpose flour
- 1 teaspoon vanilla extract
- 3 large eggs
- 2 teaspoons ground cinnamon
- Nonstick cooking spray
- 4 ounces dark chocolate, chopped
- ¼ cup Greek yogurt

Directions:

1. In a medium saucepan over medium-high heat, combine the water, butter, and the 1 tablespoon of sugar. Bring to a simmer. Add the flour, stirring it in quickly. Continue to cook, stirring constantly, until the mixture is thick, about 3 minutes. Transfer to a large bowl.
2. Using a spoon, beat the flour mixture for about 1 minute, until cooled slightly. Stir in the vanilla, then the eggs, one at a time.
3. Transfer the dough to a plastic bag or a piping bag. Let the dough rest for 1 hour at room temperature.
4. Insert the Crisper Basket and close the hood. Select AIR CRISP, set the temperature to 375°F, and set the time to 30 minutes. Select START/STOP to begin preheating.
5. Meanwhile, in a medium shallow bowl, combine the cinnamon and remaining ½ cup of sugar.
6. When the unit beeps to signify it has preheated, spray the basket with the nonstick cooking spray. Take the plastic bag with your dough and cut off one corner. Pipe the batter directly into the Crisper Basket, making 6 churros, placed at least ½ inch apart. Close the hood and AIR CRISP for 10 minutes.
7. Meanwhile, in a small microwave-safe mixing bowl, melt the chocolate in the microwave, stirring it after every 30 seconds, until completely melted and smooth. Add the yogurt and whisk until smooth.
8. After 10 minutes, carefully transfer the churros to the sugar mixture and toss to coat evenly. Repeat piping and air crisping with the remaining batter, adding time as needed.
9. Serve the churros with the warm chocolate dipping sauce.

Pear And Apple Crisp

Servings: 6 | Cooking Time: 20 Minutes

Ingredients:

- ½ pound apples, cored and chopped
- ½ pound pears, cored and chopped
- 1 cup flour
- 1 cup sugar
- 1 tablespoon butter
- 1 teaspoon ground cinnamon
- ¼ teaspoon ground cloves
- 1 teaspoon vanilla extract
- ¼ cup chopped walnuts
- Whipped cream, for serving

Directions:

1. Select BAKE, set the temperature to 340°F, and set the time to 20 minutes. Select START/STOP to begin preheating.
2. Lightly grease a baking pan and place the apples and pears inside.
3. Combine the rest of the ingredients, minus the walnuts and the whipped cream, until a coarse, crumbly texture is achieved.
4. Pour the mixture over the fruits and spread it evenly. Top with the chopped walnuts.
5. Place the pan directly in the pot. Close the hood and BAKE for 20 minutes or until the top turns golden brown.
6. Serve at room temperature with whipped cream.

Appendix A: Measurement Conversions

DRY MEASUREMENTS CONVERSION CHART

3 TEASPOONS = 1 TABLESPOON = 1/16 CUP

6 TEASPOONS = 2 TABLESPOONS = 1/8 CUP

12 TEASPOONS = 4 TABLESPOONS = 1/4 CUP

24 TEASPOONS = 8 TABLESPOONS = 1/2 CUP

36 TEASPOONS = 12 TABLESPOONS = 3/4 CUP

48 TEASPOONS = 16 TABLESPOONS = 1 CUP

METRIC TO US COOKING CONVERSIONS

OVEN TEMPERATURES

120 °C = 250 °F

160 °C = 320 °F

180° C = 350 °F

205 °C = 400 °F

220 °C = 425 °F

LIQUID MEASUREMENTS CONVERSION CHART

8 FLUID OUNCES = 1 CUP = 1/2 PINT = 1/4 QUART

16 FLUID OUNCES = 2 CUPS = 1 PINT = 1/2 QUART

32 FLUID OUNCES = 4 CUPS = 2 PINTS = 1 QUART

 = 1/4 GALLON

128 FLUID OUNCES = 16 CUPS = 8 PINTS = 4 QUARTS = 1 GALLON

BAKING IN GRAMS

1 CUP FLOUR = 140 GRAMS

1 CUP SUGAR = 150 GRAMS

1 CUP POWDERED SUGAR = 160 GRAMS

1 CUP HEAVY CREAM = 235 GRAMS

VOLUME

1 MILLILITER = 1/5 TEASPOON

5 ML = 1 TEASPOON

15 ML = 1 TABLESPOON

240 ML = 1 CUP OR 8 FLUID OUNCES

1 LITER = 34 FL. OUNCES

WEIGHT

1 GRAM = .035 OUNCES

100 GRAMS = 3.5 OUNCES

500 GRAMS = 1.1 POUNDS

1 KILOGRAM = 35 OUNCES

US TO METRIC COOKING CONVERSIONS

1/5 TSP = 1 ML

1 TSP = 5 ML

1 TBSP = 15 ML

1 FL OUNCE = 30 ML

1 CUP = 237 ML

1 PINT (2 CUPS) = 473 ML

1 QUART (4 CUPS) = .95 LITER

1 GALLON (16 CUPS) = 3.8 LITERS

1 OZ = 28 GRAMS

1 POUND = 454 GRAMS

BUTTER

1 CUP BUTTER = 2 STICKS = 8 OUNCES = 230 GRAMS = 8 TABLESPOONS

WHAT DOES 1 CUP EQUAL

1 CUP = 8 FLUID OUNCES

1 CUP = 16 TABLESPOONS

1 CUP = 48 TEASPOONS

1 CUP = 1/2 PINT

1 CUP = 1/4 QUART

1 CUP = 1/16 GALLON

1 CUP = 240 ML

BAKING PAN CONVERSIONS

1 CUP ALL-PURPOSE FLOUR = 4.5 OZ

1 CUP ROLLED OATS = 3 OZ 1 LARGE EGG = 1.7 OZ

1 CUP BUTTER = 8 OZ 1 CUP MILK = 8 OZ

1 CUP HEAVY CREAM = 8.4 OZ

1 CUP GRANULATED SUGAR = 7.1 OZ

1 CUP PACKED BROWN SUGAR = 7.75 OZ

1 CUP VEGETABLE OIL = 7.7 OZ

1 CUP UNSIFTED POWDERED SUGAR = 4.4 OZ

BAKING PAN CONVERSIONS

9-INCH ROUND CAKE PAN = 12 CUPS

10-INCH TUBE PAN = 16 CUPS

11-INCH BUNDT PAN = 12 CUPS

9-INCH SPRINGFORM PAN = 10 CUPS

9 X 5 INCH LOAF PAN = 8 CUPS

9-INCH SQUARE PAN = 8 CUPS

Appendix B: Recipes index

Brussels Sprout
Honey-sriracha Brussels Sprouts 50

Butternut Squash
Rosemary Roasted Squash With Cheese 58

C

Cabbage
Spicy Cabbage 60

Carrot
Nut And Seed Muffins 12

Cashew
Rosemary Baked Cashews 67

Cauliflower
Cauliflower Steaks With Ranch Dressing 49
Spicy Cauliflower Roast 51
Sriracha Golden Cauliflower 53

Cheese
Everything Bagel Breakfast Bake 6
Everyday Cheesecake 83

Chicken
Fried Buffalo Chicken Taquitos 21
Simple Whole Chicken Bake 21
Lettuce Chicken Tacos With Peanut Sauce 28
Grilled Cornish Hens 30

Chicken Breast
Chicken Breakfast Sausages 7
Stuffed Spinach Chicken Breast 20
Lemon Parmesan Chicken 24
Buttermilk Ranch Chicken Tenders 26
Spiced Breaded Chicken Cutlets 28
Dill Chicken Strips 29
Potato Cheese Crusted Chicken 31
Blackened Chicken Breasts 31
Crispy Chicken Parmigiana 32

Chicken Drumstick
Spicy Bbq Chicken Drumsticks 26
Sweet-and-sour Drumsticks 29

Chicken Thighs
Sriracha-honey Glazed Chicken Thighs 30
Lemon And Rosemary Chicken 31

Chicken Wing
Crispy Dill Pickle Chicken Wings 23
Soy-garlic Crispy Chicken 23
Maple-teriyaki Chicken Wings 24
Buttermilk Marinated Chicken Wings 66

Chocolate
Rich Chocolate Cookie 78
Chocolate And Coconut Cake 78
Chocolate Coconut Brownies 79
Black Forest Pies 84
Ultimate Skillet Brownies 86
Churros With Chocolate-yogurt Sauce 87

Coconut Milk
Coconut Brown Rice Porridge With Dates 12

Cod Fillet
Crispy Cod Fingers 68

Corn
Corn Pakodas 51
Creamy Corn Casserole 55
Maple Butter Corn Bread 72

Cremini Mushroom
Mushroom And Onion Frittata 18

D

Duck
Glazed Duck With Cherry Sauce 27

E

Eggplant
Double "egg" Plant (eggplant Omelets) 59

F

Firm Tofu
Black-pepper Garlic Tofu 59

Flank Steak
Miso Marinated Steak 42

Flour
Fast Coffee Donuts 16

G

Graham Cracker
Graham Cracker Cheesecake 82

Green Olive
Breaded Green Olives 64

Ground Turkey
Turkey And Cauliflower Meatloaf 22
Turkey Meatballs With Cranberry Sauce 25
Mini Turkey Meatloaves With Carrot 27
Turkey Stuffed Bell Peppers 32

H

Ham
Brown-sugared Ham 36

Hazelnut
Orange And Anise Cake 77

I

Italian Sausage
Grilled Sausage Mix 10
Bacon-wrapped Stuffed Sausage 38

J

Jack Cheese
Cheesy Apple Roll-ups 70

K

Kale
Spicy Kale Chips 67

L

Lamb
Garlic Herb Crusted Lamb 46

M

Mozzarella Cheese
Mozzarella Meatball Sandwiches With Basil 38

Mushroom
Spinach, Leek And Cheese Frittata 11
Pork Chops With Creamy Mushroom Sauce 36
Balsamic Mushroom Sliders With Pesto 50
Cheese And Ham Stuffed Baby Bella 73

O

Orange
Baby Back Ribs In Gochujang Marinade 34

P

Peach
Caramelized Peaches 68
Curry Peaches, Pears, And Plums 86

Pecan
Chocolate Pecan Pie 81
Candied Pecans 82

Pie Crust
Fudge Pie 79

Pineapple
Pineapple And Chocolate Cake 79
Rum Grilled Pineapple Sundaes 83

Pork
Spicy Pork With Candy Onions 41
Simple Pork Meatballs With Red Chili 43
Pork Spareribs With Peanut Sauce 45

Pork Belly
Lechon Kawali 34

Pork Chop
Vietnamese Pork Chops 39
Pork Chops In Bourbon 40
Ranch And Cheddar Pork Chops 44
Apple-glazed Pork 45

Pork Loin
Herb And Pesto Stuffed Pork Loin 37

Pork Loin Chop
Tonkatsu 42

Pork Sausage
Sausage Ratatouille 35

Pork Tenderloin
Honey-caramelized Pork Tenderloin 39
Crispy Pork Tenderloin 40

Potato
Fried Potatoes With Peppers And Onions 14
Potato And Prosciutto Salad 39
Honey-glazed Roasted Veggies 56
Garlic Fries 63
Sweet Potato Chips 66
Sweet Potato Fries With Honey-butter Sauce 70

Prosciutto
Prosciutto Mini Mushroom Pizza 57
Crispy Prosciutto-wrapped Asparagus 62

Pumpkin Puree
Pumpkin Pudding 81

R

Ricotta Cheese
Grilled Egg And Arugula Pizza 9

S

Sausage
Queso Bomb 65

Scallop
Bacon-wrapped Scallops 35

Shishito Pepper
Grilled Shishito Peppers 70

Sirloin Steak
Sweet And Tangy Beef 41

Skirt Steak
Beef And Scallion Rolls 37

Spinach
Spinach With Scrambled Eggs 8
Spinach Omelet 9
Creamy And Cheesy Spinach 53

Squash
Summer Squash And Zucchini Salad 54
Cheesy Summer Squash With Red Onion 67

Strawberry
Cinnamon Toast With Strawberries 7
Mixed Berry Dutch Baby Pancake 8

Swerve
Blackberry Chocolate Cake 80

T

Tomato
Bruschetta With Tomato And Basil 72

Turkey Breast
Strawberry-glazed Turkey 20
Rosemary Turkey Breast 22
Turkey Jerky 25

Turkey Thighs
Roasted Cajun Turkey 21

Z

Zucchini
Grilled Vegetable Pizza 56
Simple Ratatouille 60

Printed in Great Britain
by Amazon

24107925R00053